Anita Dobson was born in Stepney, in the heart of London's East End. She went to school there and still lives within a mile of her birthplace. Since leaving drama school in 1970, she has performed in numerous stage roles, ranging from Shakespeare to pantomime, as Magenta in the *Rocky Horror Show*, as Kitty in *Charley's Aunt*, and on television in many plays and series, as a regular presenter on BBC TV's *Playaway* and in Thames Television's *Up the Elephant and Round the Castle*.

From 1985 to 1988, Anita Dobson appeared as Angie Watts in *EastEnders*, which became the most popular television series of all time, regularly watched by over 20 million viewers – half the population of Great Britain!

In August 1986, Anita's first record, 'Anyone Can Fall In Love', reached No. 4 in the pop charts, earning her a silver disc. Also in 1986, she received the PYE Award as TV Actress of the Year and the *TV Times* Actress of the Year Award. She has become one of the best-known and most written-about personalities in Britain. *My EastEnd* is her first book.

ANITA DOBSON

MyEastEnd

SPHERE BOOKS LIMITED

FOR MY FAMILY

SPHERE BOOKS LTD

Published by the Penguin Group
27 Wrights Lane, London W8 5TZ, England
Viking Penguin Inc., 40 West 23rd Street, New York, New York 10010, USA
Penguin Books Australia Ltd, Ringwood, Victoria, Australia
Penguin Books Canada Ltd, 2801 John Street, Markham, Ontario, Canada L3R 1B4
Penguin Books (NZ) Ltd, 182–190 Wairau Road, Auckland 10, New Zealand

Penguin Books Ltd, Registered Offices: Harmondsworth, Middlesex, England

First published by Pavilion Books Ltd in association with Michael Joseph Ltd 1987
Published by Sphere Books Ltd 1988

Designed by Lawrence Edwards

Printed in Great Britain by
Butler & Tanner Ltd, Frome and London

Contents

Introduction

MY East End! 'How presumptuous!', you would be entitled to think. How can I possibly claim a whole chunk of London as mine? So let me start by saying that the East End is mine in the same way as one speaks of *my* school or *my* country, in the sense of belonging to it. It's especially true of the East End, because belonging is my principal feeling, as it is of thousands of other East Enders for whom this particular part of London means far more than just a geographical area.

Many large cities have an 'East End', all of which have a distinctive character. At the beginning of my professional acting career, I worked in repertory in Glasgow, and lived in that city's East End, the Gorbals. New York's Lower East Side has the same sort of background of poverty and deprivation, and a pattern of immigrant groups not dissimilar to London's East End.

It may be hard for outsiders to understand how anyone can possibly feel affection for the East End. Much of it is dirty and ugly. About a third of it was wiped out during the Blitz – and a lot of what went up to replace it is not pretty. Most of its people were poor – many still are – and it has had a long history of trouble, from the racial conflicts of the 'thirties to the Krays' gangland murders. It is not by accident that Whitechapel Road is the cheapest property in Monopoly!

Yet there is another, more positive side to the coin: alongside the derelict sites and the grim tower blocks the East End contains many of London's most interesting old buildings, and even some of the best modern ones. Its pubs, its docks and its bustling markets, such as Petticoat Lane, are known the world over; and, something that's particularly close to my heart, it has a unique place in the history of British theatre: the first London theatre was built there when Shakespeare was still at school, and the music hall tradition, and many of its greatest performers, have their origins in the East End.

More than all this, it's the people that make the East End what it is: East Enders not only produced a language all their own – Cockney, with its unique rhyming slang, but they are famed for their humour, which grew out of their reaction to their poverty – 'snatching wit from want' as it has been described. They are noted too for their willingness to make the best of any situation: their resilience in times of adversity was seen at its height during the Blitz, but continues even today.

East Enders are quick-witted – what today would be called 'street-wise' – and hard working, with a determination to get the job done. They are warm-hearted and generous: in the face of hardships and sorrows, the East End has been the very cradle of compassion – both Dr Barnardo's and the Salvation Army were established there – and traditional values of the best sort have created communities based on close family ties and a community spirit that is unmatched in any large city.

East Enders are proud of *their* East End and have never thought of themselves as in any way inferior to any other Londoners: 'Your true Cockney is your only true leveller,' wrote William Hazlitt. 'Let him be as low as he will, he fancies he is as good as anybody else.' Here is a story that illustrates his pride:

In the 1920s, the London telephone exchanges were being converted so that instead of calls being connected via the operator, you had to dial the first three letters of a name, followed by the number. Sometimes the names were the actual names of the areas, but often the numerical equivalent was unusable for some reason – HAMpstead and HAMmersmith, for example, were identical, so only one of them could use the 'HAM' prefix. When it came to issuing the East End exchange names, Mile End was given the progressive-sounding 'ADVance' and Poplar the simple 'EASt', but when it came to assigning a name to the Wapping exchange, there was a problem: the numerical equivalent of 'WAP' was not available. Despite the fact that very few people in Wapping even had a telephone, they were outraged! It was as if their name had been given away! They were offered numerous alternatives and turned them all down as unacceptable. Eventually, a clever GPO official suggested 'ROYal' – which was accepted, so that this, one of London's most poverty-ridden areas, acquired one of the grandest of all telephone names!

I must make the point that there are, as it were, two East Ends. There is the traditional East End of pre-war generations, with its overcrowded housing, poverty and deprivation, at its very worst in the nineteenth century but continuing right up to the last war. This is the East End my parents knew, and which they have frequently described to me. Then there is the post-war East End, the East End of my generation: a great deal of the slums Hitler's bombs did not succeed in destroying, local authorities swept away and replaced with tower blocks, and with them went most of the extremes of poverty. My East End has its roots firmly in the East End of the past, and it's important to be aware of one's roots – but it would be a mistake to confuse the two. When I describe the old East End, I am reporting what I have read or what I have been told by people who knew those times.

Every week, an astonishing number of people watch *EastEnders*. As a member of the cast, I would say that the programme presents an honest picture of real East End life, but no drama series can possibly convey what it means to have been brought up there, the area's historic associations or its significance in the lives of its inhabitants. I was born in the East End, and I have lived there for most of my life. As a result, I feel a sense of identity with the place and its people. In the pages that follow, I hope I have succeeded in conveying to you some of my enthusiasm for my birthplace, the place I love – my East End.

Anita Dobson
Wapping, E1, 1987.

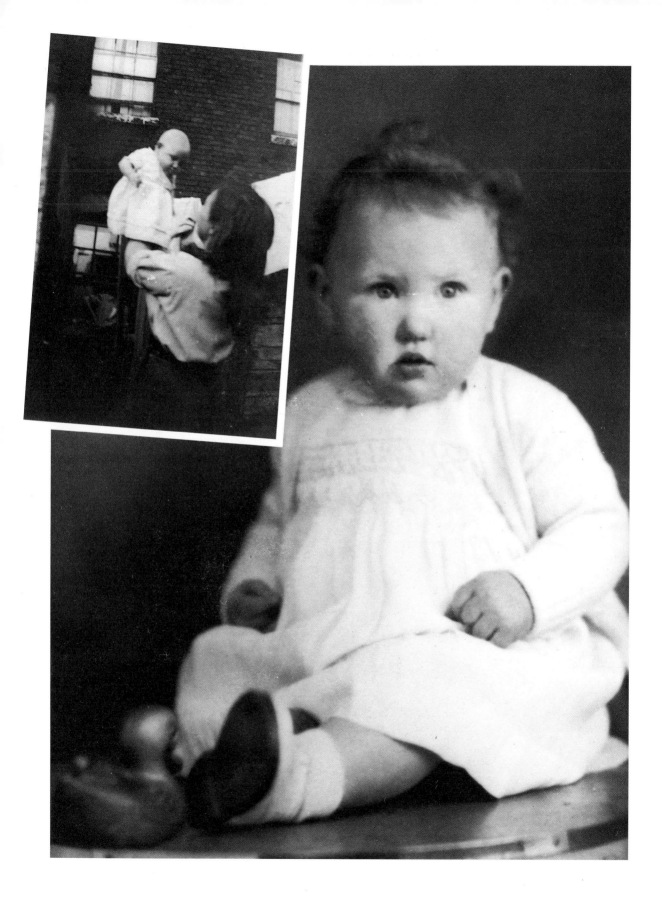

An East End Kid

Growing up in the East End

ONE OF my earliest memories is of rabbits. I was about three. We had recently moved out of my Nanna's house in Rhodeswell Road, Limehouse, but the family was having one of its frequent get-togethers there. I was dog-tired but held out as long as I could, then Mum took me upstairs and put me down to sleep on the sofa. The party carried on downstairs, to the sound of the old wind-up gramophone. Perhaps it was this noise that woke me up. In the twilight, I looked around the room and saw them – a family of tiny rabbits scampering about! I watched them, fascinated, until Mum came upstairs.

'Shhh!' I whispered. 'You'll scare the rabbits!'

'Rabbits?' Mum asked, puzzled. 'There's no rabbits here, dear.'

'Yes there are,' I told her, 'look,' and she followed my pointing finger.

'Oh, my god!' she screamed, 'They're *mice*!' And she scooped me up and whisked me out of the room.

Like so much else in the East End, the house is no longer there – today its site is just a patch of grass between the Mile End Stadium and the Grand Union Canal. Looking across the canal, I could see the newly-built flats in Maroon Street, four-storey blocks put up to replace the houses bombed during the Blitz, when about a third of all the property in the East End was destroyed. I often wondered what it would be like to live there – and, as fate would have it, I was to do so some years later. If the flats symbolised the post-war generation, then my Nanna's house was a reminder of the housing of the original East Enders. Not only did it suffer from invasions of 'rabbits', and had creaking floorboards, but it lacked the basic amenities that we all take for granted today: there was an outside loo, and even an outside brass tap and drain where Nanna used to peel vegetables under the icy running water – and where too my Uncle John, my Aunt Ivy's husband, used to

The best-fed kid on the block! An early pose, and Mum and me in the back garden at Rhodeswell Road.

11

strip to the waist and wash as best he could after a day's work. A more comfortable arrangement was the tin bath in the living room, filled with water heated on the stove in kettles and saucepans.

I was born in the Bancroft Road Ḥospital, off the Mile End Road, in the heart of the East End – one of the first National Health babies in what had formerly been the local 'Poor Law Hospital' – and spent the first three years of my life in Nanna's house. Living quite literally on top of each other, like almost everyone else in the East End, there was inevitably always a sense of belonging both to a family and to a wider community. I remember as a small child that the doors were never locked and family and neighbours often popped in. I also recall that I was prevented from popping *out* by the presence of a barred gate across the front doorway. I ingeniously overcame this problem by hanging over the gate, soliciting to passing children by offering them pieces of fruit. As a result, though the fruit bowl was often empty, I acquired lots of friends!

Next door lived Mr Carlaw, who kept chickens in his garden. In ours, my grandfather – Bill to everyone – cultivated roses. There was also a lilac tree. I remember Bill mending the family's shoes there, hammer in hand, with cobblers' nails bristling from his mouth – and me dreading that he would swallow them! The house backed onto the canal, and beyond the wall of the little garden was the towpath. It remains a working canal, but when I was a child the barges were still being towed by horses, and I could climb up the back wall and watch them lumbering past, just a few feet away. It was a fascinating sight for any child, but a strictly forbidden place to play – despite which all the local children, myself included, congregated there.

As a child, I first became aware of the sights and sounds of the East End when I was taken to the Waste, the market held in Mile End Road on a Saturday morning. Going 'down the market' was a real occasion then, and I used to dress up in my Sunday (or Saturday) best. I was always well dressed, so it appeared that we had more money than we really did. This was a perk of my Dad's job. One of the youngest of a family of nine, his father had died when he was four. His Mum lived on until her nineties, still enjoying her glass of Guinness at the local. Dad was in the army during the war, and was injured. He had aspirations toward the stage (a family trait, evidently, since my great grandfather on my mother's side had been a singer and pianist), and after he was demobbed thought of entering a repertory company. As he couldn't afford the admission fee, he ended up instead in the rag trade as a cutter for a dress factory in Middlesex Street, where Petticoat Lane market is held. He held this job for nearly 30 years until the company closed, a victim of the

Below: Mum and Dad – and they're still kissing!

Opposite: Some of the many faces of Anita Dobson.

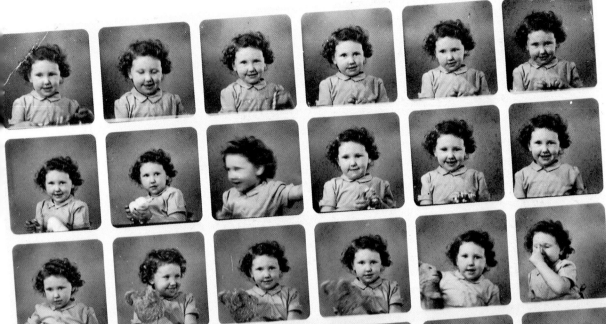

Above left; With Nana and Bill.
Above right: The chocolate-box kid.

Opposite: The regulation school photograph, showing the Dobson grin.

growth of the high street chain stores. While he worked there, he was able to cut the clothes that Mum used to make up at home, creating for me a wardrobe that was second to none.

When I was three, Mum and Dad got a modern council flat, 27 Stothard House, Cephas Street in Stepney, and it was in Cephas Street that I first went to school. The John Scurr Primary School is a forbidding-looking Victorian building behind a high wall – but my abiding memory of it is as a happy place. I loved everything about it – the plays we acted, the games we played, and especially the wonderful teachers who encouraged us to *want* to learn. My Mum did dinner duty there, later becoming a teaching assistant at Frank Barnes, a school for deaf children. Not long after I started to appear on television, I received letters from my form teacher, Douglas Hobbs, and from Mr Jones, my former headmaster, who asked, 'Could it be that the girl I see in *EastEnders* is the same auburn-haired girl from our school?' Yes, it was me! I went back to the school recently. It's hardly changed: the little coat-pegs are still there, and it smells exactly the same. It's acquired a tiny training pool for infant swimmers, and the whole place is beautifully decorated with colourful murals, including one depicting major events in the history of the East End, such as the Siege of Sidney Street and the Blitz. Throughout the school, work done by the children is displayed and the whole place has an air of love and enthusiasm just as I remember it from 30 years ago!

Out of school, I used to play in the street or on a local derelict site known as 'The Debris', with the other kids from the local flats. We were allowed to stay out until dark as long as Mum knew where we were – and usually we were within calling distance anyway. Among our games, 'Tin Tan Tommy', rounders and 'Knock Down Ginger' (knocking on doors and running away) were perennial favourites. 'Kiss Chase' was also popular. Like a game of tag in which boys chase girls and, when they catch them, are allowed to kiss them, it was my first experience of the strange ways of boys. Why, I wondered, did the same boy always catch me? Why did the boy I really liked never catch me? These were mysteries to be solved as I got older.

Family gatherings were regarded as the highlights of life in the East End. My mother's side of the family was particularly close, and as well as get-togethers at Nanna's, we often spent Christmas at my Aunt Ivy's – my mother's sister who had moved to the Lansbury Estate in Poplar. The Lansbury is a model estate built as the 'live architecture' exhibition for the 1951 Festival of Britain and named after George Lansbury, the MP and leader of the Labour Party in the 'thirties. Lansbury was not only influential in politics, fighting on a 'Votes for Women' platform and founding the *Daily Herald*: he was also the man who pioneered public bathing in the Serpentine in Hyde Park, and he was the father of the actress, Angela Lansbury. My parents were not great pub-goers, but visits to Aunt Ivy's invariably involved a trip to the local, the Lord Stanley. Though newly built, its atmosphere was that of a traditional East End pub, where every night was talent night, with all the regulars getting up to sing. It was usually the least talented or drunkest who put on the best entertainment, and it was all good fun – though I remember sitting there dreading that someone might ask me to perform!

Poplar has another claim to fame: it was there in 1919 that a local Methodist minister, W.H. Lax, invented the street party, to celebrate the end of the First World War. Street parties became special favourites of East Enders – I still treasure my photograph of the party for the Coronation in

Left: Me and my cousin Paul at the seaside.

Opposite: An early solo performance with the Ivy Travers troupe – Mum made the dress.

1953, held at Kirk's Place, opposite Rhodeswell Road. There we all are in our best clothes and party hats, munching our way through mounds of sandwiches – under cover, as my abiding memory of the day is that it poured with rain! Another of my photos shows me at a birthday party – minus my front teeth! The tooth fairy used to come and leave 6d under my pillow. This was later increased to a shilling – that's fairyland inflation for you!

Sunday dinner was the main meal of the week. It was always a roast, and you could smell it cooking throughout the flats. Preparing dinner was, of course, Mum's allotted task, but, unusually, in our family my grandfather also cooked. Bill had lost a leg, but determined not to become a chairbound cripple, he dedicated himself to perfecting the art of baking the most wonderful cakes and pastries. Two weeks before my birthday, he gave me a birthday cake which I carried home on the bus. 'Why did he give it to me so much in advance?' I wondered. Not long afterwards, he went quietly to his bedroom, lay down and passed away.

I used to listen to the radio as a child – especially Radio Luxembourg, noted for the dreadful quality of its signal, which had the annoying habit of fading away in the middle of a record. I remember the adverts, the first we ever heard on the radio – but to this day, I ask myself, 'Who *was* Horace Batchelor of Keynsham, spelt K-E-Y-N-S-H-A-M, Bristol?' We had our first television in our flat in Cephas Street. It was a black and white set, of course. I remember being particularly fascinated by the fact that its seemingly gigantic screen was concealed behind a pair of doors. Among my favourite programmes were *Muffin the Mule*, *The Flowerpot Men* and *Andy Pandy*. But more even than them I adored *Rag, Tag and Bobtail*. I especially loved the voice of the man who said, 'Hello Rag. Hello Tag. Hello Bobtail,' and I loved the little garden in which they lived, which reminded me of my Nanna's garden – and she had 'rabbits' too! Whenever there was anything a bit scary on TV, I used to hide behind the table, peeping out with one eye covered; if it was something *really* frightening, such as *Quatermass*, I actually hid *outside* the room, peeping through the crack in the door!

My Dad never owned a car – nor, as far as I know, did any of my friend's parents – and we rarely travelled outside the East End. I went on holidays with the school to the Isle of Wight, and as a family we went to Warner's Holiday Camp, where I was proudly enrolled as a 'Warner's Wagtail' and sang a song in the talent contest, which I won – much to Mum and Dad's delight!

On Saturday mornings I used to go to the ABC Cinema at Stepney Green. The Saturday morning pictures was the best excuse for getting noisy kids out of the house, so that they could run riot in the cinema from 10.00 to 1.00, screaming and throwing things at each other, with boys tweaking the girls' hair. Everyone of my generation fondly remembers the cartoons and the old black and white *Flash Gordon* serials which starred Buster Crabbe.

When I was older, on Saturday mornings, while Mum did the weekly wash and looked after my little sister, I used to do the shopping at the small parade at the end of the street, in turn visiting the butcher, the

At the Coronation party, Kirks Place. I'm the little one, second from the left at the front – with her legs crossed!

Early acrobatics with the Ivy Travers troupe – I'm the nervous one, third from the right.

Nana, with me (at the back) and my cousins, on the landing at Stothard House, Cephas Street.

greengrocer and the grocer's. Supermarkets were only starting to appear, and we did not have one near us. Some of the old-time street traders, such as rag and bone men with horsedrawn carts and knife grinders used to call at the flats, but it was the ice-cream man who interested us most. When he arrived, you would hear the cry go up along the street, 'M-u-u-u-m!' followed by windows opening and mothers' heads appearing with the response, 'Wot?!' Then a few coins, wrapped in paper, would be tossed out of the window, to be squandered on a threepenny ice-cream or a toffee apple. We were especially lucky in Rhodeswell Road, for not far away was Tiani's, a shop that sold traditional Italian ice-cream, the most delicious I have ever tasted. He also sold another favourite of mine, Jubblies – pyramid-shaped frozen orange drinks – as well as sweets like flying saucers, shrimps, sherbert dips, penny chews, blackjacks, gobstoppers, liquorice bootlaces and sweet cigarettes. At our corner shop at the end of Cephas Street, I also bought comics – *Beezer*, *Beano* and *Dandy*. The memory of such characters as Desperate Dan, Biffo the Bear, Korky the Cat, the Bash Street Kids and Dennis the Menace lives with me still, and I would like to state here, in writing, that if Dennis Potter ever writes a screenplay for a 1950s children's comic story, I *insist* on being cast as Beryl the Peril! I was also a fan of the American 'Superhero' comics such as *Superman* – and like so many other children of my generation, I curse the fact that I did not save these comics, many of which are now rare collectors' items. I'm sure my love of science fiction must date from these and the Saturday morning pictures with *Flash Gordon*: to this day I am a sucker for the TV re-runs of *Twilight Zone*.

A demure shot of me in the playing fields at Rhodeswell Road – now the Mile End Stadium.

Like many kids in the East End, even though money was scarce, I was well-loved – spoiled, even, to the extent of Mum and Dad's means. I can never remember going without, and I know that everything they earned went on the table and our clothes, with what little was left being put aside for Christmas and birthdays. Presents were simple but always fun, and usually there was one 'big' present and lots of little ones. One Christmas I had a complete Mambo Band, consisting of a triangle, a tambourine, pieces of sandpaper to rub together, maracas, a kazoo and blocks of wood. I recruited the whole family into Anita's Mambo Band – and a dreadful racket we made too! Another Christmas I had a magic set, with a wand, a wizard's hat and a selection of amazing tricks, and puzzles made of interlocking pieces of wire and indoor fireworks that uncoiled like snakes – and made a horrible stink! I was seriously into teddies and furry toys, but like all little girls I also had to have a doll. She was a baby that blinked and had a pram of her own. I tried to get her to sit at a desk I had, but she

The girl most likely to? Collecting a school prize – dress by Mum.

slipped off and cracked her head open. Mum said, 'Don't worry', and took her to the local doll's hospital to be patched up. It's a telling thought that even though poverty and hardship were rife in the East End, in the midst of all this there were obviously sufficient Mums and Dads who cared enough for their kids' happiness to support a doll's hospital.

The best present I ever had was a red Raleigh bike. Mum and Dad warned me for weeks before Christmas that I was not to be too disappointed if they found they couldn't afford it, because bikes were terribly expensive – but, of course, they somehow managed it. I spent most of Christmas with Dad teaching me to ride it in Bethnal Green Gardens – which we called 'Barmy Park' because so many seemingly crazy people used to frequent it! I used to keep it in the pram shed at the bottom of the flats, with no fear of it being stolen. In those days, too, the flats had not been vandalised or invaded with aerosol-spray graffiti: the most serious wall decorations consisted of chalked hearts, with

22

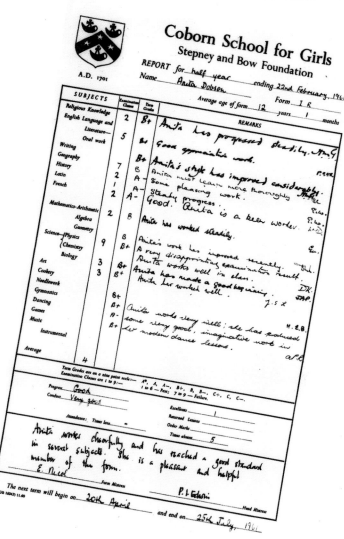

declarations like 'PM L AD'. I remember my sister, who is nine years younger than me, being born when we lived at the flats. When she was very tiny, to our horror, she vanished. Every inhabitant of the flats turned out in a mass search for her – until she was eventually found, having gone 'visiting' a neighbour.

One of the few memorable crises that affected my otherwise trouble-free childhood was when I stepped into the lift at the flats. The doors closed, but I was too small to reach the button. I stood there in tears, terrified, until my Dad found me. I never entered the lifts again. At the age of eleven, I had appendicitis and was operated on at the Queen Elizabeth Hospital for Children, Hackney Road. When I was discharged, Mr Hobbs arranged for the class to visit me in our tiny flat. When I came home, Mum and Dad had fitted my bedroom out with my first grown-up bedroom suite – a sign that I was no longer a little girl, but a young woman.

The whole family was under the marvellous medical care of an elderly doctor of the old school, Dr Depla – the sort of doctor who would call round, day or night. When he was due to retire, his son started to take over the practice, but all the older generation of East Enders continued to ask to see *old* Dr Depla, until they finally accepted that the son was every bit as skilled as his father, and accepted him as *their* doctor.

I took the 11-Plus and got a scholarship to Coborn Grammar School for Girls, Bow, among whose famous pupils of the past are Deborah Creditor (later Lady Gaitskill) and the entertainers Elsie and Doris Waters, the sisters of Jack 'Dixon of Dock Green' Warner. This was regarded as something of an achievement, as would it have been had I gone on to University – though even more so in my Dad's day: he described the success of one of his contemporaries who actually succeeded in getting a University place as a phenomenon on the same scale as climbing Mount Everest!

Unlike John Scurr, Coborn was concerned with getting pupils through exams. I started out all right, and was top in Latin and good at history and English, but as the terms went by, my enthusiasm for academic subjects dwindled. I also hated the uniform and repeatedly tried to lose my Panama hat. I also believe now – though whether I was aware of it at the time I am not sure – that single-sex schools are not a particularly good thing. Going to an all-girls school and then suddenly discovering boys can prove a terrible shock to the system!

Sadly, neither music nor drama was featured prominently at my secondary school though I did play in *The Merchant of Venice* – Shylock in class and Portia in the school production. Outside school, the East End music hall tradition lived on in a much diminished form. When I was very tiny, I had been taken to a pantomime at the People's Palace, Mile End Road. I loved every minute of it, and danced in the aisles. I was desperate to go to the toilet, but held on so that I wouldn't miss any of the show or have to use a strange loo. When I got home, Mum plonked me on the toilet, where I sat, legs swinging, singing all the songs from the show. My interest in acting developed and we often staged impromptu shows on the steps of the flats. The theatre soon had its grip on me, and – especially when he had a win at the Hackney greyhound races – Bill would treat us to the Friday night variety shows at the Queen's Theatre, Poplar. I remember we once had a box, and we won a bowl in a raffle: I nearly fell out of the box with excitement! When I was four, I performed with a juvenile group, singing, appropriately, 'They Tried to Tell Us We're Too Young'. By the age of five I had enrolled in the Ivy Travers dance troupe (Ivy was a relative of Ben Travers, the farce playwright) which performed at the York Hall Swimming Baths in Old Ford Road. I also appeared as Alice in the John Scurr production of *Alice in Wonderland*. By eleven I was attending Saturday morning drama classes at Toynbee Hall in Commercial Street. Toynbee Hall was founded in 1884 as a voluntary organization with its declared aim being 'To educate citizens in the knowledge of one another, to provide teaching for those who are willing to learn and recreations to those who are weary'. I had my first taste of 'proper' acting there, playing such parts as Cecil in *The Queen and Mr Shakespeare*. It

Mum and her teenage daughter on holiday.

was also my first experience of the power of acting, when I realised the thrill of the audience reaction to a funny line.

Soon after I left school, there was some suggestion that I should take up acting professionally, but I told my Mum, 'I want to be ordinary'. I duly did all the things that ordinary girls did: I left school at 16 with four O-levels, and worked as a clerk at the head office of the Prudential Assurance Company in Holborn. I got engaged to the boyfriend I had for four years, and I was well on my way to getting married and producing children when I suddenly thought, as in the words of the song, 'There's got to be something better than this!' So I told my Mum, 'I've changed my mind. I want to be *extra*ordinary!' I enrolled with the Bertha Myers Company at the Toynbee Hall Myrdle Street annexe and in August 1968 we went on tour in Czechoslovakia – my first trip abroad – where we presented, largely in the form of mime, a visual picture of London. Unfortunately, while the Czech people appreciated this hands-across-the-sea gesture, the Russians chose the precise moment of our debut to send troops into the country – but that's another story.

My East End

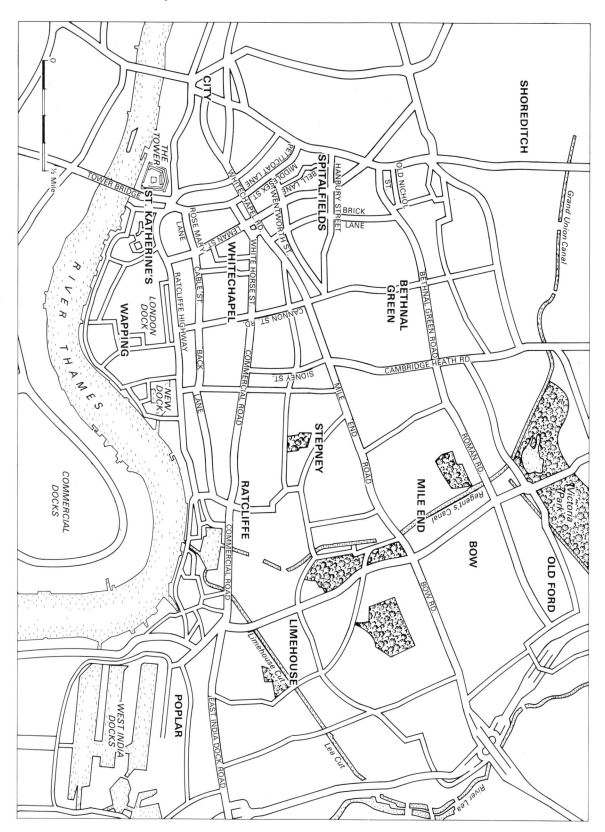

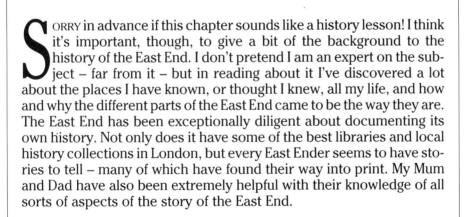

The Story of The East End

S ORRY in advance if this chapter sounds like a history lesson! I think
it's important, though, to give a bit of the background to the
history of the East End. I don't pretend I am an expert on the subject – far from it – but in reading about it I've discovered a lot
about the places I have known, or thought I knew, all my life, and how
and why the different parts of the East End came to be the way they are.
The East End has been exceptionally diligent about documenting its
own history. Not only does it have some of the best libraries and local
history collections in London, but every East Ender seems to have stories to tell – many of which have found their way into print. My Mum
and Dad have also been extremely helpful with their knowledge of all
sorts of aspects of the story of the East End.

THE EAST END VILLAGES

Starting at the beginning, it's hard to imagine, since the East End is so
built up nowadays, that it wasn't all that long ago that parts of it were
really quite rural – though names like Bethnal Green and Spitalfields
give a hint of their earlier character. Writing about Stepney in 1504,
Thomas More said, 'Wherever you look, the earth yieldeth you a pleasant prospect – here you find nothing but bounteous gifts of nature.'
It's certainly changed a bit since then! I've always wondered why St
Mary's church, Bow, is stuck in the middle of nowhere (actually next to
a modern flyover!). The reason is that it used to be a village church on
a village green.

WHITECHAPEL HAY MARKET 1788

The heart of the East End was **Stepney**. It got its name from the Saxon *Stebunhithe*, or 'Stebba's landing place' – though no-one is sure who Stebba might have been. In medieval times it was the manor of the Bishops of London. They even had a palace with extensive grounds: the palace was demolished and in 1845 the grounds became Victoria Park. The parish of Stepney was once a huge heath and included virtually the whole of the East End, from the edge of the City in the west to the River Lea in the east, and from Bethnal Green in the north to the Thames in the south. St Dunstan and All Saints church in Stepney High Street was once the church of this huge parish and is the only church that is almost entirely medieval in the East End. It is still the church that Stepney residents go to – I was once a bridesmaid there.

At the time of the Domesday Book (1086), Stepney was entirely rural, with meadows and woods and a population of just 900. It was steadily built up after the sixteenth century, and 100 years ago the population was nearly 300,000, many of them immigrants, and Stepney became synonymous with poverty and overcrowding. Stepney became a for-

Whitechapel Hay Market – the plaque dates from 1888, but shows the scene 100 years earlier.

28

Trams in Whitechapel High Street, 1929.

mal borough in 1900. The Blitz altered everything: thousands of houses were destroyed and the population dropped to less than 100,000 after the last war.

The Borough of Stepney, along with Bethnal Green and Poplar, became Tower Hamlets in 1965. Although this was a new local authority, the hamlets had been recognised as an area for hundreds of years: they were the 21 villages that comprised the East End and which supplied men to the militia based at the Tower of London. Gradually, the villages grew up and acquired individual characters.

Whitechapel was once just a small hamlet in the gigantic parish of Stepney. Its name comes from the fact that in the thirteenth century, it acquired a chapel built with white stone. Whitechapel was, according to eighteenth-century historian John Strype, '. . . a great thoroughfare, being the Essex Road and well resorted unto, which occasions it to be the better inhabited and accommodated with good inns for the reception of travellers, and for horses, carts, coaches and wagons'. The Whitechapel Road was the main route from Essex and the East of

England into London – and it is still well served by many pubs. Well into this century, herds of cattle were driven along it and wagons used to lumber down it, bringing cartloads of hay for London's huge population of horses. That's why it is one of the widest streets with the broadest pavement in London – the only way pedestrians could avoid the mud splashed up from the carts. If you peep inside the doorway of the Whitechapel Library, there is a panel of brightly-coloured tiles with a picture of the hay carts. It's 100 years old, and the scene it shows is 100 years older than that, but it must have been like that for centuries. The hay market was actually closed in 1928, but the Hayfield Tavern in Mile End Road and Hayfield Passage are further reminders of this old

Above: Toynbee Hall, the scene of my early amateur dramatics – the original building.

Right: The Whitechapel headquarters of the Salvation Army.

trade. My Dad told me that even up to the Second World War, cars were relatively rare in the East End: the police had them, and a handful of individuals, and lorries were seen increasingly, but the average family never dreamed of being able to afford a car. Pre-war photos show kids playing safely in East End streets without a car in sight.

As well as being a thoroughfare, Whitechapel became a centre for noisy and smelly industries, such as metal foundries, sugar refineries and fish-curing plants, because they were banished from the City of London, and in the Victorian period it was the centre of the East End's Jewish population and the location of cheap lodgings for dockers.

Toynbee Hall, to which – as I have already mentioned – I owe a great

debt for the part it played in my drama training, opened in 1884. It was named after the social reformer Arnold Toynbee, but actually founded by Canon Samuel Barnett, the vicar of St Jude's. It has been responsible for over a century of important social and other work in the East End. The Youth Hostel Association started there and the Whitechapel Art Gallery was launched in the building. The theatre was practically destroyed in the Blitz, but reopened in 1964 – just in time for me to start taking classes there!

Mile End – so-called because it was once marked with a milestone indicating that it was one mile from the City of London – was a common in the medieval period. King Edward I held a parliament in 1299 at Mile End Green, and a palace was later built on the site. It was on the common that peasants from Essex gathered during the Peasants' Revolt in 1381. By the sixteenth century Mile End was already overrun with tumble-down buildings, and gradually became the home of weavers and other craftsmen. It has also always had nautical connections: the very pretty Trinity Almshouses which still stand in Mile End Road were built in 1695 by Sir Christopher Wren for '28 decayed masters and commanders of ships or widows of such', and the explorer, Captain James Cook, lived in a house on the site of 88 Mile End Road. Mile End grew rapidly in the Victorian period, and although it was always thought of as being relatively respectable – at least when compared with the squalor of Bethnal Green – it suffered from a good deal of poverty: within two years of each other Booth started the Salvation Army in Mile End and Dr Barnardo began his charitable work among homeless children.

Another East End institution, the London Hospital, was founded in Mile End in 1740. It grew steadily and became an important medical school. One of the strangest cases it must have handled was that of John Glascott, who in April 1842 was taken in after his leg had been broken – by an elephant! He had been visiting a fair in Commercial Road, and had teased the elephant. When he returned later, it wrapped its trunk round his leg; serious complications later developed, and Glascott died. He should have known that elephants never forget! Coincidentally, it was the London Hospital that cared for Merrick, the unfortunate person who was known as 'the Elephant Man', rescuing him from being exhibited as a freak. This was soon after Queen Victoria had opened a new wing of 'The London' in 1876, which made it for many years the largest hospital in England.

Queen Victoria returned to Mile End in 1887 to open the People's Palace, another institution, like Toynbee Hall, that was built with the education and recreation of the poor in mind. Unlike the traditional East End music halls, it was never really popular – probably because it attempted to provide working people with 'highbrow' entertainment, which did not interest them. In 1931 it was burned down, was rebuilt three years later, but was as unsuccessful as its predecessor. It was acquired by Queen Mary College in 1953 and became part of London University.

Spitalfields seems like a very strange name until you discover that the 'spital' part is like the 'spital' in 'hospital' – and indeed in Medieval

Christ Church, Spitalfields – once used by Huguenot silkweavers.

Following pages: Spitalfields Market in 1928.

Fashion Street: the centre of today's East End rag trade.

times there was a hospital and priory called St Mary Spital, on the site of Spital Square. Most of the area was open fields up until the seventeenth century, cultivated by people like Nicholas Culpepper, the famous herbalist, who lived in Spitalfields in the 1640s. The very first Baptist church in the whole of England had been built here in 1612, and Christ Church Spitalfields was designed by the great architect Hawksmoor. What made Spitalfields really famous, though, was its silk weaving and, at a later date, the production of other expensive cloths. Although the industry, run mainly by French immigrants, declined early in the nineteenth century, it left a wonderful legacy in the form of the weavers' Georgian houses, which are some of the best in London and nowadays 'highly desirable', as estate agents say. Just visit Fournier Street and look at the doorways and the other decorative details on the houses, and you can imagine what these streets must have looked like two hundred years ago. Nearby, at 56A Artillery Lane, is perhaps the best preserved eighteenth-century shopfront in London. Ironically, it is now the premises of a computer company, but they have maintained its appearance perfectly.

Spitalfields Market in Commercial Street is a wholesale vegetable market dating back to the seventeenth century. New buildings were created in the nineteenth century and it was rebuilt in the 1920s. It has always seemed to me a very uninteresting area, but now, like the other old London wholesale markets such as Covent Garden and Billings-

gate, it is due to be redeveloped, so maybe it will become the East End's Covent Garden.

Brick Lane is so-called because bricks and tiles were once made in the area. Truman's brewery occupies a large stretch of the street: they have tacked a very space-age looking building, all glass and stainless steel, onto their old premises, but surprisingly enough, the result is quite effective. Most of the rest of the street seems to be occupied by Indian rag trade workshops and what must be the greatest concentration of Indian restaurants in London. The Rivoli Garage is on the site of the blitzed Rivoli Cinema, itself built on the site of the oddly-named 'Wonderland', an old boxing ring.

East Enders are never sure whether Hackney is or is not part of the East End: in some ways it seems to belong to it, but its houses are larger and its inhabitants were always better-off than those in the rest of the East End. Let's not argue, but say it's on the border. Even though it is now part of Hackney, **Shoreditch** seems very much an East End 'village'. St Leonard's in Shoreditch High Street is thought of as an East End church. It was founded in the twelfth century and, since Shoreditch was once a centre of the woodworking trade, the church has many fine carvings. More unusually – and more evidence for the former village character of the East End – it still has a whipping post and village stocks in the churchyard! What I find really interesting about it is that it has a lot of theatrical associations: Will Somers, Henry

Truman's Brewery, Brick Lane: a blend of old and modern.

VIII's court jester, was buried here in 1560, as were Gabriel Spencer, an actor who was killed by playwright Ben Jonson in a duel in 1598, and Richard Burbage, the actor-manager and friend of Shakespeare's, whose father James built London's first theatre nearby.

The Geffrye Museum is in Kingsland Road, Shoreditch. Just before the First World War, it was created out of 14 early eighteenth-century almshouses that had been built by Sir Robert Geffrye, Lord Mayor of London in 1685 – hence the name of the museum. It contains furniture from different periods in room settings. You can walk through them all, so it's like being a time traveller as you pass from one to another.

Bethnal Green's name is a puzzle: some people say it comes from the Saxon 'Blida's Corner' (another of those mystery East Enders!) or from 'Blithehale', *blithe* meaning happy and pleasant (as in 'Blithe Spirit'), and *hale* a retreat, or maybe it's from Bathon Hall, after a family called Bathon who lived there during the reign of Edward I. It was on the ancient Roman route from the City to East England – hence the name Roman Road – and many Roman remains have been found here. Bethnal Green was once an actual green – Bethnal Green Gardens ('Barmy Park' – the place where I learned to ride my bike, if you recall) is all that remains of the village green. The area was quite rural up to the eighteenth century – the sort of place where wealthy Londoners had country houses. One rather unpleasant inhabitant was Edmund Bonner, Bishop of London in Tudor times. He lived in the Bishop's palace here, and in Queen Mary's reign, in what came to be called 'Bonner's Fields', he burned Protestants at the stake. He ultimately died in jail, but his ghost was said to haunt Bethnal Green once a year, riding three times round Bonner's Fields in a black coach. Anyone who got so much as a glimpse of him died!

A hundred years later, in 1666, Samuel Pepys escaped from the Great Fire of London – dressed in his nightgown. He loaded up a cart with all his most valuable possessions and travelled to Bethnal Green to stay with Sir William Ryder at his huge mansion, Kirby's Castle (later Bethnal House Lunatic Asylum). Bethnal Green and adjoining Haggerston were once fashionable places for the country houses of such people as Edmund Halley, who gave his name to Halley's Comet, and William Caslon, the famous printer, who retired to Bethnal Green in about 1758.

In the eighteenth century many silk weavers and dyers moved from Spitalfields, which was becoming overcrowded, into the south west part of Bethnal Green, which itself then became very built up and over-crowded: in 1743 there were said to be 1,800 houses and 15,000 inhabitants! When the weaving industry declined in the nineteenth century, other poorly-paid domestic industries replaced it, such as furniture-making (there are still a number of firms involved in the trade, such as the veneer companies in Redchurch Street), shoemaking and clothing. By the Victorian period, Bethnal Green had become one of London's poorest locales. A report of 1868 stated that 'A large part of the population, at the best of times, is on the verge of pauperism', and by 1889 it was reckoned that 45 per cent of the population was living below subsistence levels. As a measure of the relative poverty of the area, at this time annual rents in Mayfair averaged £150; in Bethnal Green they

Then and now: Street games in Shoreditch, 1928, and picnicking in the gardens off Cambridge Heath Road.

were £9. It was the area round Old Nichol Street that Arthur Morrison used as the setting for his 1896 novel, *A Child of the Jago*, a fictionalised but mostly accurate picture of the criminals who inhabited this part of the East End. After the publicity generated by this book and other accounts of the dreadful poverty of the area, a certain amount of slum clearance took place. The 'Old Nichol' was swept away and new apartments built on the site. The Boundary Street Estate, the roads radiating out from Arnold Circus, with its incongruous bandstand, largely cover what had been a rabbit-warren of dark alleys populated by London's most notorious villains. In this century, the population of Bethnal Green declined from its peak of 130,000 in 1901 to 58,000 by 1951. Its notorious poverty is well within living memory: as recently as 1945, 89 per cent of the houses in Bethnal Green had no bathrooms.

Victoria Park – officially in Hackney, but much used by East Enders – is a 290-acre park opened in 1845. It has always been popular: I used to go there to the boating lake or paddling pool, and Dad used to swim there in the open-air baths built in 1936. The park contains all sorts of oddities, including stone alcoves from the old London Bridge and a Chinese pagoda from a Victorian exhibition which was re-erected on an island in the boating lake.

Angela Burdett-Coutts (1814-1906), heiress to the Coutts banking fortune, spent enormous sums of money on worthy philanthropic

Mums and kids in the Bethnal Green Museum of Childhood.

causes in the East End. She also involved herself in several rather dotty schemes: one of them was to erect a gigantic elaborate drinking fountain in Victoria Park. In view of the poverty all around, especially on the Bethnal Green side of the park, a 60-foot high drinking fountain seems a bizarre waste of money. (In complete contrast, just outside the park, in Lauriston Road, is a much more down-to-earth little drinking fountain inscribed with the sweet message, 'From L.S. and B.S. 1881. To commemorate 25 years of happy married life'.) Baroness Burdett-Coutts also applied her well-meaning charity to another large-scale plan for the people of Bethnal Green. Believing that poor East Enders were being cheated in the old street markets, she spent vast sums on building the Columbia Market. Described as 'one of the great follies of the Victorian Age', it was a huge two-acre covered market building resembling a cathedral and adorned inside with signs and slogans like 'Be sober, be vigilant, be pitiful, be courteous'. It was opened in 1869, was a financial disaster (probably because East Enders preferred their street markets), and was closed and demolished between 1958 and 1966, when flats were built on the site. Looking at pictures of it, you can see what a monstrosity it was – no wonder that East Enders hated it!

The building I have always loved in Bethnal Green, however, is the Bethnal Green Museum of Childhood. It has the best collection of dolls in the country, as well as toys, model theatres, puppets, costumes – especially wedding dresses – and other treasures. It also has exhibits relating to the old Spitalfields silk industry. It's always popular, but especially on Sunday when whole families go there and you can see the children with their faces pressed against the cases of toys and dolls' houses, gazing in wonder.

On the Cranbrook Estate, off Old Ford Road, there is a statue of a beggar and a dog by the modern sculptor, Elizabeth Frink. It depicts

High-spirited East End outings between the Wars.

Henry de Montfort, 'the blind beggar of Bethnal Green'. Henry, the son of Simon de Montfort, was blinded at the Battle of Evesham in 1265. Legend has it that, though of noble birth, Henry became a beggar, and his daughter Bessie worked as a barmaid at the King's Arms, Romford. When suitors discovered her father was a beggar, all of them turned away except a knight. He married her and at their wedding feast Henry appeared, threw off his rags and gave them £3,000. Windfalls like this were not exactly something that happened every day in the East End, short of winning the pools, so you can imagine the impact of the legend! A more recent building, York Hall Baths and Assembly Rooms in Old Ford Road, dating from 1929, is of special importance to me – it is one of the first places I acted in.

The River Lea, which has been navigable since the 1820s from Hertford to the Thames at Limehouse, was crossed by a ford – hence the name of **Old Ford**. My Dad's family came from Old Ford. Most of it has been swept away by redevelopment since the war, but Old Ford Road still has some interesting relics of the old community: Netteswell House, a seventeenth-century building, remains intact, and at No. 288 a blue plaque commemorates Israel Zangwill, the author of an East End classic, *Children of the Ghetto*. A more recent building, York Hall Baths and assembly rooms in Old Ford Road, dating from 1929, is of special importance to me – it is one of the first places I acted in.

The bridge at **Bow** improved the river crossing – its name comes simply from the bow shape of the old stone bridge, which is said to have been built by Queen Matilda, wife of Henry I. Like a lot of the East End, this was once a rural area where Londoners went to savour the countryside: Pepys wrote in his *Diary* on 11 June 1664: 'With my wife only to take ayre, it being very warm and pleasant, to Bowe and Old Ford; and thence to Hackney. There light and played at shuffle board, eat cream and good cherries; and so with good refreshment home.' There was even a palace known as Bromley-by-Bow Palace – which was demolished in 1893, though one beautiful room from it was saved and can be seen in the Victoria and Albert Museum. In the eighteenth century Bow became famous for calico printing and Bow porcelain. It was also infamous for the Bow Goose Fair, once held at Whitsun on a site off Fairfield Road; it degenerated into such a drunken orgy that it was banned early in the nineteenth century. My connection with Bow is, of course, that I attended Coborn School – which, with its 'brother', Coopers' School, has now moved to Upminster.

A lot of people outside the East End are very confused about Bow Bells, so here's the story: Everyone knows that you can only be a real Cockney if you were born within the sound of Bow Bells, and they know from the nursery rhyme, 'Oranges and Lemons', about 'the great bell of Bow'. Most people know that there's a place in the East End called Bow, so they assume that it was the bells of St Mary, Bow, that are referred to – but it wasn't! It was another St Mary, known as St Mary-le-Bow in Cheapside, in the City of London. From medieval times, a curfew was rung on the 'great bell of Bow' at 9 pm every day, so people in the City and the adjoining East End would have heard it. The bells were made at the Whitechapel Bell Foundry, but were destroyed when the church was gutted by bombing in the Blitz. It has been rebuilt, but the new bells were not installed until 1961. This means that technically anyone born between 1941 and 1961 can't claim to be a Cockney! Unfortunately, that includes me – but I'm not bothered by this minor technicality: as far as I'm concerned, I'm a Cockney, born and bred!

Until very recently a strange custom used to take place on the first Saturday of each month at the Fern Street Settlement in Bow: 'Farthing Bundles' containing small presents – toys, puzzles, beads and so on – were distributed to children small enough to walk under a special arch. Not long ago hundreds would turn up, but in recent years so few children could be bothered that the custom, which was started as a weekly event in 1907 by a charitable organisation, was abandoned. One interesting fact about this old custom is that over the years, as their diets and environment have improved, East End kids have got progressively taller for their age. As a result, the organisers had to raise the arch by four inches to ensure that enough children qualified!

Poplar was named after the poplar trees that once grew there, but which were all cut down by the early eighteenth century. Its country character disappeared when the docks were built, and docking and shipbuilding became the dominant industries. It was here, in Napier Yard, that Brunel's *Great Eastern* was built in 1858 – the largest ship ever built up to that time. Poplar was also the headquarters of the East

Children queuing for their 'Farthing Bundles' – more popular in the pre-war period than in recent times.

India Company. Sadly, it was its very proximity to the docks that destroyed so much of Poplar – over half its houses were damaged or destroyed in the Blitz, and it now consists mainly of modern council housing.

Limehouse is named not, as some books say, because there were lime trees growing here, or because limes were warehoused here, but after the lime kilns around the docks: chalk was brought from Kent and burned in the kilns to be used in making mortar for London's building industry. The Regent's Canal, opened in 1820 to link the Grand Union Canal with the Thames and docks, runs from Paddington to Limehouse. It was the Limehouse stretch of the canal that ran behind my grandparents' house in Rhodeswell Road, and which, when I was a child, was still quite active. I particularly remember seeing barges laden with timber.

Charles Dickens knew Limehouse well and often wrote about it. He used to come here to visit his godfather, Christopher Huffam, who lived near St Anne's, in Church Row (now Newell Street). The church of St Anne, Limehouse, is said to have the highest clock in London. The churchyard contains a mysterious pyramid: a tomb, perhaps? If so, whose? Nobody seems to know. Other authors wrote about Limehouse and made it famous – or infamous. A Chinese community settled here in the late nineteenth century, most of them sailors or employed in the local docks. They were largely law-abiding and kept themselves to themselves, never mixing much with the East Enders, but a small group of them attracted a lot of publicity when various Victorian investigative journalists exposed the fact that they were operating opium dens. Once the story got around, the British public assumed that every Chinaman was an opium addict or a white slaver. In Oscar Wilde's only novel, *The Picture of Dorian Gray*, Dorian goes to Limehouse to obtain opium, and Fu Manchu, Sax Rohmer's oriental villain, or his evil henchmen are often up to no good in Limehouse. Even today, the Chinese influence is still present in Limehouse – in the form of some very good Chinese restaurants!

Other nearby East End 'villages' include **Ratcliff**, between Wapping and the Isle of Dogs, which was once the most densely populated part of Stepney, and **St Katharine's**, where the Royal Hospital was founded in 1149. The Dock opened in 1828, and has recently undergone the most dramatic transformation of any part of the East End to become a very popular tourist spot.

Wapping is said to have got its name from yet another of those unknown characters – 'Waeppa'. Wapping High Street and Wapping Wall were noted for their taverns, some of which survive, and for Execution Dock, which doesn't. That was the place where pirates were once hanged. It used to be an incredibly rough, tough area, noted for its inns and drunken sailors. Dr Johnson suggested that people who explored Wapping would see 'such modes of life as very few could even imagine'. Nowadays Wapping resembles a gigantic building site with new riverside developments that range from up-market flats converted from disused warehouses to the *Times* and other newspaper headquarters. And my present home!

*Left: Sixty years ago:
Docklands children
making friends with
the local vicar,
Riverside Mansions,
Wapping.
Below: Docklands
today.*

THE IMMIGRANTS

A clue to the cosmopolitan variety of produce to be bought here is furnished by the names over the shops; names of colour and character. They carry you all over England, and all over Europe and parts of Asia. Here is a random selection: Pommerantz, Frumkin, Yallop, Toporovsky, N. Decent, Wing Moy, A'llchild, Eastwind, Longue-haye, Pinkus, Skyline, Spielsinger, Proops, Suliman, Mirza Feros, Iraboona, Domb, Travell, Sowerbutts, Agombar, Yaker, Suss, Kareem, Sugarbroad, Chestopal, Oldschool, Summercorn, Devo, Petrikoski, Cheek, Fergus, Stockfish, Scampino, Rooney, Yenush, Bonallack, Ox, Sam Shu Lee, Sonabend, Mohammed, Chunder Dut, Filipe.

So wrote Thomas Burke in his 1932 book, *The Real East End*. Living in the East End, no-one could fail to notice just how amazingly cosmopolitan it was. Nowhere in Britain has experienced such huge waves of immigration, nor so many of them: French Huguenots, Germans, Irish, Jews, Chinese, West Indians, Indians – each group has introduced its own industries and stamped its own individual character onto the area in which it has settled. They were in the East End because it was near the docks – as in New York, where many immigrants, having arrived, never went beyond Manhattan.

London had always attracted strangers – tradespeople who for one reason or another had chosen to or been forced to leave their own countries. The first major influx, though, took place in 1685. Huguenots – French Protestants – had been more or less tolerated in France up to that year; then the law (known as the Edict of Nantes) that allowed them to live, work and worship there, was revoked. Fearing the sort of massacres that had befallen them in the past, most of them fled – as many as 100,000 of them coming to England.

They were hard-working, religious and honest, and so they were generally accepted into the communities into which they settled. A large number were artisans involved in the silk-weaving industry, and they settled in Spitalfields – close enough to the wealthy City of London to have a ready market for their products on their doorstep. Soon what had been a largely rural area was built over with weavers' houses – some of which can still be recognised by their large skylights, which provided the workrooms with enough light to work by. At one time, there were at least 15,000 weavers working at their looms here. Mulberry Street in Whitechapel was so called because they grew mulberry trees on which to rear silkworms.

Dennis Severs, an eccentric American resident of Spitalfields (18 Folgate Street, E1), has devised an unusual way of enabling people to discover what life would have been like for a Huguenot weaver. He has completely restored his eighteenth-century house. Visitors spend an evening there, experiencing the sights, sounds and even the smells of

Right and below: East End charity – the Soup Kitchen for the Jewish Poor, yesterday and today.

Opposite: 1950s immigrants in Cable Street.

the house, with tape-recordings of the sort of conversations that might once have taken place there.

The Irish followed on the heels of the Huguenots: from the middle of the nineteenth century, emigration from rural Ireland occurred on a huge scale. Many of them went to the United States, setting up Irish-American communities in New York, Boston and other cities. They also came to England in great numbers, taking work in the expanding canal and railway building industries and in the East End docks. Because they were often willing to accept wages at a lower level than the English, there were often anti-Irish protests in the East End.

There had been Jews in London for centuries, many of them in the East End. Most of them were engaged in the clothing and other trades. They were noted for their charity among their widows, orphans and any of their number who was down on his luck. After 1881 Jewish refugees started coming to England from Russia and Poland. The trickle soon became a flood, and in the years up to about 1905 huge numbers arrived, many of them at Irongate Stairs near St Katharine's Dock, from where the majority walked the mile or so into the heartland

of the Jewish East End. They created a serious problem of overcrowding, but they also brought with them many benefits: they imported their own cuisine – their bakeries, delicatessens and restaurants, which are still found throughout the East End, their own trades and shops – particularly those involved in mass-produced clothing, like the firm for which my Dad used to work – and their culture. The first Yiddish theatre in London was at 3 Princelet Street. Fanny Waxman's Yiddish Theatre operated in Adler Street from 1936. Adler Street, off Whitechapel Road, was itself named after a prominent Jewish East Ender, Chief Rabbi Hermann Adler. Many Jewish artists and intellectuals grew up in the East End, such as Israel Zangwill, author of *Children of the Ghetto*, and Jacob Bronowski, as well as many notable left-wing politicians, among them Mannie Shinwell.

Many Jewish immigrants became wealthy. Some stayed in the East End, others moved on to the Jewish suburbs of London, such as Golders Green. Some went further afield to seek their fortunes. Barney Barnato, a penniless East End immigrant, tried his luck in the diamond fields of Kimberley, South Africa. He rapidly became a multi-millionaire, rivalling Cecil Rhodes, who finally bought him out in 1889 with a cheque for £5,338,650! (Barnato actually returned to London – but committed suicide on the voyage!) Not all hit the big time though: the Soup Kitchen for the Jewish Poor still exists in Brune Street near Petticoat Lane.

The way in which the immigrant groups changed, almost from one generation to the next, is exemplified by a single building on the corner of Brick Lane and Fournier Street in Spitalfields. It was built in 1742 as a Huguenot chapel. With the decline of the Huguenot community it was taken over by Methodists in 1809. In 1897 it was converted into a synagogue, and in 1975 it became a mosque for the Bangladeshi community.

East End Muslims at the Mosque, Whitechapel Road.

THE EAST END IN THE NEWS

The Ratcliff Highway Murders

In the nineteenth century, Ratcliff Highway was a notorious area – the words of an old song warned sailors to 'mind Ratcliff Highway and the damsels loose'! Most crimes were robberies, until a series of seven brutal murders shook London: on 7 December 1811, Mr Marr, a shop-keeper, and his wife, child and assistant were found butchered; then, on the 11th, the landlord of the King's Arms, Mr Williamson, his wife and a servant were found dead with terrible wounds. The chief suspect in the Ratcliff Highway Murder Case, a sailor called John Williams, was arrested on slim evidence, but on 15 December hanged himself before he could be brought to trial. He was buried on 30 December 1811 according to an old custom – at a crossroads, where Cable Street joins Cannon Street Road, with a stake through his body – probably the last occasion this was carried out in London. When gas mains were being excavated in August 1886, his remains were found.

The Princess Alice

On Tuesday 3 September 1878, *The Princess Alice*, a 251-ton pleasure steamer, was returning from a trip to Sheerness. On board were over 700 passengers (there was no passenger list, so numbers are uncer-tain), many of them East Enders enjoying a day out. At about 7.40 pm at Gallions Reach she collided with *The Bywell Castle*, a 1,376-ton steamer, and sank immediately. Around 200 people were saved, but 16 of them died later. At least 550 drowned – 120 of them were buried in Woolwich Cemetery. The scale of the calamity – particularly as so many of the dead were women and children – stunned Victorian London and virtually destroyed the Thames pleasure boat business. A woman called Elizabeth Stride claimed that she had lost her husband and her children in the tragedy, and in her desperation took to drink and the streets. She was to become the second victim of Jack the Ripper.

Jack The Ripper

In 1862 a survey of part of Whitechapel by the Association for the Sup-pression of Vice found that of 656 houses, 166 were brothels! Even in my day I can recall people telling me that certain parts of the East End were well-known haunts for prostitutes. Whoever Jack the Ripper was, his grudge was directed against such women, and the viciousness of his attacks – and the fact that he was never caught – have made him London's most famous murderer. All five of his victims were East End prostitutes, killed and mutilated within a few streets of each other in the Whitechapel area between September and November 1888. No-one was ever brought to justice, but speculation as to the identity of the

'Ripper' has continued for nearly a century, and ranges from a deranged freemason to Queen Victoria's grandson, the Duke of Clarence. The Ghost of Annie Chapman, murdered in Hanbury Street, is said to haunt the street. The Jack the Ripper pub, then called the Ten Bells, is an authentic Victorian establishment where victim number five, Mary Kelly, was last seen alive. A morbid list of the Ripper's victims is displayed in a window.

Poverty and Charity

According to Walter Besant, two million East Enders had 'no institutions of their own to speak of, no public buildings of any importance, no municipality, no gentry, no carriages, no soldiers, no picture-galleries, no theatres, no opera – they have nothing'. Whether or not the lack of opera concerned many East Enders, their lack of adequate food and housing did. The deprivation was so great and so obvious that throughout the nineteenth century the East End was *the* area for charitable causes. George Peabody (who has the distinction of being the only American buried in Westminster Abbey) built his first 'Peabody Trust' houses for the poor in Commercial Street, Spitalfields, in 1862-64. A year later, William Booth founded the Salvation Army, opening its first headquarters in Whitechapel Road in 1867. Irish-born Thomas Barnardo planned to become a medical missionary in China, and was studying at the London Hospital. He was so appalled by the poverty he saw all around him, especially among children, that in 1867 he started his Home for Destitute Boys at 18 Stepney Causeway, with the slogan, 'No Destitute Child Ever Refused Admission'. He bought the Edinburgh Castle, a pub and music hall in Poplar, converting it into a Coffee Palace and Mission Hall. These were the beginnings of Dr Barnardo's Homes.

East End Politics

The anti-poverty campaigners did what they could to relieve the social problems of the East End. Political activists tried to do the rest. The East End has always been a stronghold of radical causes. The Chartists, an electoral reform movement, assembled in 1848 in Victoria Park. Karl Marx's daughter Eleanor organised trades unions in Whitechapel. Lenin visited Whitechapel in the early years of this century, as did Stalin, Trotsky, Prince Kropotkin and various other Russian revolutionaries. The East London Federation of Suffragettes was founded

Opposite: The list of Ripper victims at the Jack the Ripper pub.

Below: Statue of William Booth, founder of the Salvation Army, on Whitechapel Road.

in Bow by Sylvia Pankhurst, and Gandhi stayed at Kingsley Hall in Powis Road in 1931 – the occasion was commemorated with a blue plaque.

Two words of political jargon were invented in the East End: 'Poplarism' was the name given to the practice of providing relief to the poor on an extravagant scale, after the Borough of Poplar had done so in 1919. David Lloyd-George was noted for his fiery speeches in Limehouse in 1909 – and thus the word 'Limehouse' came into use to describe any inflammatory speech. (More recently it has become associated with the Social Democratic Party (SDP), the leader of which, David Owen, lives in this newly fashionable part of London.)

The East End's Labour allegiance has always been very strong and obvious. John Scurr, after whom my primary school was named, was MP for Stepney. George Lansbury, Labour MP in 1910-12 and 1922-40 and leader of the Labour Party from 1931-35, lived at 39 Bow Road, where there is now a memorial garden dedicated to him. Dad remembers him well: he had a benign appearance and great public appeal. He often walked through East End streets like the Pied Piper, followed by crowds of children singing a rhyme into which they slotted the name of the current opponent:

Vote, vote for Mr Lansbury
Kick old ---- out the door.
Lansbury is the man
Who gives us bread and jam –
So we won't vote for ---- no more!

Clement Attlee was Secretary of Toynbee Hall before becoming mayor of Stepney, and MP, succeeding George Lansbury as leader of the Labour Party and becoming Prime Minister in 1945. In the same year, Mile End had the East End's first Communist MP.

Anyone interested in East End politics should pay a visit to the National Museum of Labour History which is in Limehouse Town Hall. Harold Wilson, then Prime Minister, opened it in 1975 – donating to it one of his famous pipes! It also contains trade union banners, relics of East End strikes, such as the Match Girls', and other Labour mementoes.

The Siege of Sidney Street

On 3 January 1911 the police believed they had tracked down two members of a gang of foreign anarchists, one of whom was thought to be the notorious 'Peter the Painter', to 100 Sidney Street. A policeman who knocked on the door was shot; 400 further armed police, members of the Scots Guard, Royal Engineers and the Fire Brigade – as well as Winston Churchill who was then Home Secretary – promptly descended on the house, and the Siege of Sidney Street began. It did not last long: at 1 pm the house caught fire and the two men died in the blaze. Neither of the bodies was that of Peter the Painter. He was never heard of again, and the circumstances of the Siege were never fully explained.

The Cable Street Riots

There was always some envy and resentment of the success of certain hard-working Jewish families – despite the fact that many Jews were just as impoverished as other East Enders. To capitalise on this fairly limited anti-semitism, the British Union of Fascists, known as the 'blackshirts' and led by Oswald Mosley, set up branches in the East End where they ranted against Jewish residents and their sworn enemies, the Communists. In 1936 they declared their intention to march through the East End on Sunday 4 October. An attempt to ban the march was unsuccessful, and fearing trouble, 6,000 police were mobilised. In the morning, a barricade was set up in Cable Street to obstruct the Fascists, but was soon cleared by police, and the anti-Fascist crowd that assembled was charged by mounted police – all before Mosley had even arrived near the Tower of London. By mid-afternoon, the disturbances were so serious that Mosley was asked to cancel the march, and under protest did so. The following Sunday, gangs of thugs – probably including Fascists – stormed through the East End, smashing shop windows, attacking Jews and looting shops. The Public Order Act passed soon afterwards outlawed political uniforms, such as black shirts, and the police were given the authority to ban processions. My Dad, who was in the East End at the time, said that everyone he knew did their best to avoid the riot, but clearly there was a powerful popular feeling against the marchers, and the East End was never again a target of Mosley's bully boy tactics.

Above: Winston Churchill (first top hat on the left) directs the Siege of Sydney Street, 1911.
Right: Interior of the house after the Siege.

Opposite: The Cable Street Riots, 1936.

The Blitz

Although we all grew up with people of previous generations telling us all sorts of horrendous stories about the Blitz, I was amazed to learn that bombs also fell on the East End in the *First* World War. They were dropped from Zeppelins, the first of them landing on the Swan, a pub in Bow Road. It sent a mangle flying which sadly killed the barmaid. In 1917, another fell on the Upper North Street Infants School, Poplar, killing 18 children and injuring many more.

Tragic though these incidents were, they were nothing compared with the dreadful devastation that German bombs brought to the East End in the Second World War. Between 1939 and 1945, 94,056 houses were damaged or destroyed and over 15,000 people killed in the Blitz on London as a whole, but its proximity to the docks, and the fact that bombers could use the line of the river to guide them as they flew in, meant that the East End suffered considerably more than any other part of the city.

Raids started on 7 September 1940 – 'Black Saturday' as it became known – with the docks as their specific target. They went on for 57 nights. This was the period that gave rise to the publicity about the resilience of the East Enders: two days after the start of the Blitz, under the headline, 'The Cockney is Bloody but Unbowed', the *Daily Herald* reported, 'The Cockney can take it! East London paused for a moment yesterday to lick its wounds after what had been planned by Hitler as a night of terror. But it carried on.'

Many notable buildings, including a number of churches, the London Hospital and the East End factories and breweries, were bombed, as well as thousands of houses. Dad was in the army, stationed in Surrey. He used to tell me how he'd come home on leave and see whole streets demolished, but signs up outside shops saying 'Business As Usual'. A lot of children were evacuated from the East End, which apparently made it seem strange – kids on the streets are part of life in the East End, as a writer in the *East End Observer* noted: 'Going through the highways and by-ways where our budding cricketers and footballers were wont to playfully disport themselves, not to mention the hop-scotch specialists, I missed their shrill and happy voices. The streets seemed strangely quiet.'

Dad reckoned the 'Blitz spirit' was 100 per cent accurate and was greatly impressed by the courage of the families that stayed on, sheltering night after night as bombs rained down on them in Anderson shelters and underground stations – as many as 14,000 people a night took shelter in the Tilbury Shelter under Commercial Road. There were many appalling stories; on 3 March 1943, 1,500 people attempted to get into the underground shelter at Bethnal Green, someone tripped and the people behind fell on top of each other down the staircase, killing 173 – but there were always lighter moments; there was the woman in Poplar who was having a bath when a bomb exploded. She was hurled into the street, still in her bath, which turned upside down, saving her from the flying rubble that cascaded down on her. She was

East End evacuees – though they left the Blitz behind, they still had to shelter from air raids. Here children take cover in the Kent hopfields. Life magazine described this as 'the most human picture of the War'.

Following pages: An East End Street – or what is left of it – after 'Black Saturday', 7 September 1940.

At a service in a blitzed Stepney school, East Enders commemorate the second anniversary of the Battle of Britain, 15 September 1942.

eventually rescued, shaken, stark naked and embarrassed, but otherwise none the worse for her ordeal!

After the Blitz, there was a lull, then the flying bombs or doodle-bugs started, to be followed by the V2 rockets, one of which landed on Petticoat Lane. The East End also has the distinction of receiving both the first flying bomb, which fell on Bethnal Green on 10 June 1944, and the last rocket to land on London – at 7.20 am on 27 March 1945 a V2 rocket hit two blocks of flats, Hughes Mansions in Vallance Road, Stepney, killing 124 people.

Dad has often referred to the war as the watershed between the old, traditional East End and the East End of today. It wasn't just a physical thing, with whole streets being swept away and modern blocks of flats put up in their place; it was the effect this had on community life, and the way in which attitudes changed. The pre-Blitz and post-Blitz East Ends are almost two different worlds.

East Enders

Family, community and working life

THE East End was noted for its good-looking girls. London cabbies have often said to me, 'Never mind about the West End – it's the East End that's got the best girls!' Roman Road, Bethnal Green, was a well-known 'cruising' area. Girls dressed up and paraded there with their friends, a modern version of 'promenading', but we were all so innocent. We never did more than chat and admire each other's clothes. At this time my sister used to call me 'Panda Eyes': influenced by Dusty Springfield, we used make-up that seemed to make our facial features and lips disappear – all you saw were two black eyes! Occasionally boys in cars would glide up and ask, 'Wanna ride?' The answer was always giggles followed by 'No thanks'. Some girls used to go off to the waste ground with boys, on the backs of their scooters. We thought they were brave and daring – infamous, even – but only speculated about what they got up to. I was brought up to be a 'good' girl, and not misbehaving with boys was the grown-up version of not talking to strange men or not taking sweets from a stranger.

I met my first boyfriend when I was nearly 15; he was nearly 17. I used to go to Richards, the shop at the end of the road, to get cigarettes for my Dad, and I used to see him on the way, tinkering with his Lambretta. Gradually, we got talking, and I found more and more excuses to go to the shop, getting Dad far more cigarettes than he could ever smoke! We were together for four years, and he even asked Dad for my hand – Dad embarrassing him by saying, 'I suppose you want the lot!' We saved for our marriage, and he bought me a ring, a solitaire diamond, from a little shop in Aldgate. We used to say goodnight at the door, and once we saw a shooting star, which we thought was romantic and a lucky omen.

Most of our courting was done on Mum's sofa, with Mum and Dad in the next room, so it was all very tame. We were probably the last generation for whom the possibility of a girl not being a virgin on her wedding night was never even considered – though paradoxically blokes were somehow expected to be sexually experienced. We were all very naive, but it was strangely beautiful. When an acquaintance of mine actually got pregnant, I remember my first reaction being to wonder how on earth they'd ever managed to be alone together! It was always said that if a girl got pregnant, she could get rid of the baby by drinking gin in a hot bath – though I've heard that the only thing this does is to make you very hot and very drunk! East Enders used to have big families, though by my generation they were a lot smaller than in Mum and Dad's day: those families with eight or ten kids seemed like a thing of the past. Post-war families were noticeably smaller, so people must have been using some method of birth control – but it was always a bit of a mystery, and, when I was a teenager, something of a joke. We heard stories of men going into barbers and being asked, 'Something for the weekend, guv?', or coins were handed over with a knowing wink and never a word exchanged; men hovered nervously in chemists asking to see a male assistant, or chickening out altogether and buying unwanted packets of razor blades. The very idea of condoms being spoken about or advertised on television would, I am sure, have shocked us.

Our banns were called, and we visited the vicar, who delivered the usual 'Thought for the Day' type speech about procreation, sailing forth on the sea of life, etc. I can't think we took it at all seriously, as neither of us was what you might call churchgoing. I was baptised – I still have my baptism certificate – but otherwise religion was left up to me to pursue or not, as I thought fit. On the other hand, we would never for a moment have considered marrying anywhere other than a church: like most East Enders, we wanted to do things 'properly'.

We booked the church, the reception and the honeymoon and organised the flowers. Wedding dresses were either handmade or hired. We decided to hire, and had been recommended to go to Lozner's of Muswell Hill even though this was well out of the East End – I still have the receipt! I remember Mum's uncertain reaction to seeing her elder daughter in her bridal gown. 'Very nice, dear,' she said – but I could tell her heart wasn't in it – perhaps because she instinctively knew that neither was mine.

We were both right. Something told me that there was no way I could go through with it, and the wedding was called off six weeks before the date. I realised – I think I knew all along – that I had so much I wanted to do that I wouldn't be able to do if I were married. In the East End there was – and to a certain extent still is – the assumption that wives had kids and stayed at home and looked after them and the house. This is not to say that East End men did not respect their wives – they did, often to an excessive degree: at one time, many men were too proud to let their wives work, and lived in poverty as a result. East End men were proud and, in a sense, noble: men like my father were often said to be 'one of nature's gentlemen' – that is, he was not born a gentleman, but was invariably polite in customary ways, such as holding chairs for

The old-style barber still thrives in the East End.

ladies, and not allowing anyone to swear in front of his wife.

After I'd decided against all odds *not* to do what all the other East End girls did, I threw myself into my work with the Bertha Myers group attached to Toynbee Hall, run by the Inner London Education Authority. It was an amateur company, but thought of as a good route into formal drama schools. I learned mime, dance, movement, voice control and so on. As I mentioned earlier, when I was 19 we went off to Czechoslovakia on a cultural exchange. As far as I and everyone else were concerned, the political climate there was perfectly stable, but no sooner had we arrived than the Russians moved in! We arrived in Prague and settled into our hotel just off Wenceslas Square. When we awoke the next morning, we were informed that the country had been invaded, that there were snipers in the streets and that we should keep our heads down until further notice! We immediately rushed to the windows and peered out. We heard gunfire, and shortly afterwards, when we were shepherded to another nearby hotel for breakfast, we saw lines of tanks, seemingly driven by scared-looking teenaged boys. They were as astonished by the turn of events as we were, having been told that they were on military manoeuvres, rather than occupying a

Times change, but the traditional church wedding remains the 'done thing' in the East End.

neighbouring country. I thought, 'This is not real. It's just like a film,' as we were taken past the tanks to a waiting coach. We were told not to show any favouritism toward the Czech people, or antagonism to the Soviet troops, but as the coach pulled away, we stuck our tongues out at the boy soldiers and waved flags at them.

The coach took us to Svitavy, to the east of Prague, then on to Svoyanov, a tiny place which had two shops and an hotel, where we stayed. Transport had ground to a halt and our costumes and stage sets remained at Prague railway station. As a result, our pageant of London in mime, song and sketches was performed without scenery and with us in tights and leotards – a very sparse production! The Czechs must have been totally baffled by it all, but they came night after night for two weeks, and because it was such an emotional time for them, wept a lot, hugged us and gave us endless presents.

This little excursion had taken us a long way from the East End, into East Europe! Meanwhile, back in the East End, my mother was demented. Her baby had gone away from home for the first time and was a prisoner of the Russians! What other mothers might be doing about their fledgelings she neither knew or cared – all she wanted was for me to return safely. With the grim determination for which East Enders are famous, she got onto the Foreign Office and the Czech embassy and demanded my immediate repatriation. On being politely informed by both that I was not the only British citizen in Czechoslovakia, and there was virtually nothing they could do, Mum and Dad tried to get our local MP to act and the *East London Advertiser* was advised of my plight. I was, of course, oblivious to all this. While my family were undergoing the most terrible traumas, I was having a wonderful time.

When all aliens were eventually evicted, we were shipped home by way of Vienna. There was a nasty moment when I thought I might have to leave behind my entire personal wardrobe, specially made by Mum before I embarked on my epic adventure – but it was a false alarm. As our train pulled into Liverpool Street, someone came along the corridor to tell me my Mum was waiting on the platform. She was not alone. With her was a posse of Press photographers, my bemused sister and my father, attempting to bring an atmosphere of calm to what was about to become an emotionally-charged family reunion. The *East London Advertiser* carried the story of my return from the clutches of the invading Soviet army as if I were the only East Ender to have returned safely from Czechoslovakia – and as far as Mum was concerned, I was.

Money dominated family lives – as anything does that you lack. I was never aware of how rich or poor we were. I knew that Hire Purchase – the 'never-never' – and purchase by instalments from mail order catalogues were common. Many East End families (though not ours) belonged to Christmas clubs – and even fireworks clubs – to put a little aside relatively painlessly each week – often to stop the old man spending the kids' toy money on booze. All homes that I had any contact with were rented, mostly council property. The idea of owning a home never occurred to anyone as remotely feasible. Nowadays, the

Pawnshop, Stepney – once an important feature of the lives of many East Enders.

differences between the East End lower and middle class are less obvious: like everywhere else in Britain, most people strive to live in a home of their own, to get the best possible education for their children and to have all the necessities and luxuries of life – a car, video, washing machine and holidays abroad. All things we now take for granted, but which, when I was growing up in the East End, were unheard of.

East Enders struggled and managed as best they could. The members of the family who were almost never wanting for anything were the children – parents would starve themselves first, rather than let a baby go without. East Enders were prolific knitters, so babies always had vast stocks of woollen clothes. Big, elaborate prams were also commonplace – an almost ostentatious symbol of a mother's status – and they were looked after and passed on to friends and relatives. Wearing smart clothes was similarly a sort of defence against poverty: however hard-up a family might be, a good-looking pram and well turned out girls presented the outside world with a picture of respectability.

Looking recently at the class register of my primary school was a real revelation. Not only did it remind me of so many of my old friends, but it also shows how fashions in children's names have altered through the years. Our parents, most of whom were born in the inter-war years, had the sort of solid, traditional names popular in Victorian England – Dads were all George, Edward, Joseph, William, Henry – every Tom, Dick and Harry! Mums were called Ethel, Doris, Betty, Gladys, Winifred and Edith. In Dad's day, boys' names were so often duplicated that you had to refer to someone by their full name, such as Jimmy Brown, because otherwise it was anyone's guess which Jimmy you meant.

Then you look down the column of us post-war kids: we're all called Linda, Brian, Martin, Janice, Kevin, Dennis and Jennifer. You can see the beginning of new fashions in names derived from those of film stars – Glenn, after Glenn Ford, Gary after Gary Cooper – Loraine and Roberta, and after us came all the Waynes, Traceys and Sharons. Now there seems to be a move back to the traditional names like Sarah, Emma, Victoria, John, Richard and William – though how anyone can look at a tiny baby in a cot and say, 'Let's call him Henry!' I really don't understand. Dad is Alfred and Mum is Amy (but known as Anne). They seemed to have a fondness for names beginning with 'A', and thought of names like Annabel and even Angela – so I might have been playing in *EastEnders* with my own name! I am, actually, called Ann in the family. When my sister was born, they ended the line of 'A' names and called her Gillian! East Enders always shorten names anyway – Robert is always Bob, James becomes Jim – in *EastEnders* everyone is called Flo, Bri, Col, Val, Tel, Si, Shirl, Den or Cath.

Until the last war, there was no 'youth culture' as such. Boys seemed to go straight from short trousers to suits: East End men of my Dad's generation always dressed up in suits when they went out, whether it was to go out to the local park or to the pub – casual clothes are very much part of a sense of post-war liberation, like the different names we were given, a break with a past that everyone wanted to forget.

East End families at play.

East Enders taking the air in Victoria Park.

The old East End was a very self-contained area. East Enders seldom travelled outside – people grew up, went to school, married, had children and died, often all within a few streets of where they were born. Marriages added whole new branches to already large families, and they usually lived nearby, so popping into each other's homes was common and family gatherings were frequently major affairs!

My Dad's abiding memory of his childhood is the extent to which life was lived out on the street. Houses were small, and in the days before television, there was not a lot to keep people indoors. During the summer months in particular, and on Sundays throughout the year, East End streets were thronged with people. East Enders were quite territorial and tended to keep to their 'manor': people from one East End 'village' were greeted with suspicion if they went to a pub in another, and fights often resulted. Dad has told me that it was not that East Enders were particularly belligerent – no East End man wanted to get hurt, lose a tooth or whatever, and no-one went out looking for trouble, but should it arise for whatever reason, the East Ender could take care of himself.

Dad has also explained to me how there used to be a sort of hierarchy of loyalties. The first allegiance would be to one's family, then to the street – there were often street wars between rival gangs of kids; then there would be one's school and then the area – the 'manor'; the East End itself was next on the ladder, then London, then Britain. At the very pinnacle was the Royal Family: they represented all that East

Enders most admired, and especially during the Blitz, when the King and Queen stayed in London and often visited the East End, everyone applauded them.

Women tended to age quickly in the old East End, worn out by child-bearing and the strain of coping with large families and little money. Although several members of our family were long-lived, Dad can't recall that there were many really old people: most seemed to die before they were 60, exhausted by arduous work, and their health undermined by poor housing conditions. What aged relatives the family might have were generally cared for by the family – the Salvation Army and other East End hostels for the homeless have always tended to provide shelter for vagrants and loners, rather than members of East End families. Many people tried to forget their troubles by drinking and smoking more than was good for them. When I was young, everyone seemed to smoke. In all our family photos, Dad has a ciggy in his hand; I even did it myself at Drama School, in an attempt to look cool and poised, like a Hollywood star (many of whom, of course, went on to die of lung cancer!). Now no-one in my family smokes. Respiratory problems were common in the East End, and were not helped by lack of adequate heating and by people having to wash in cold water. In an attempt to save every penny, the consumption of all manner of generally useless patent medicines was common in the days before the National Health Service enabled even the poorest East Ender, to obtain proper medical treatment.

Houses were lit by gaslight right up to the Second World War. Dad clearly remembers it from his house in Old Ford, and recalls the excitement of the arrival of the Fixed Price Electric Light Company when they installed electricity.

It is very much a part of Cockney humour to laugh at the things you can't do much about – money and lavatories therefore feature strongly in Cockney jokes. Nanna's house in Rhodeswell Road had an outside loo, which was tricky to negotiate in the dark. An aunt of mine went out there once in the night after one of Mr Carlaw's chickens had wandered in there: when she disturbed it, its squawking and the flapping of its wings in that confined space practically scared her to death! With typical British fortitude we endured hard Izal toilet paper – and I have even seen pieces of newspaper neatly threaded on string. There was, however, a certain sort of privacy about an outside loo: you could spend hours there lost in your own private thoughts. . .

Bathing in the Rhodeswell Road house was performed – and what a performance! – in the living room in front of the fire, in a tin bath filled with water from kettles and saucepans and afterwards carried outside to be emptied. It was so arduous an operation that it could scarcely be undertaken daily, so 'bathnight' was literally once a week, or people used the public baths. Somehow we managed to keep clean, however – though I remember that we had a regular nit inspection at school – and some kids were found to be infested. The bathroom in our new flat was, as you can well imagine, thought of as a great luxury.

East Enders are noted for their hospitality. As soon as anyone enters an East End household, the kettle goes on. This was especially true in

Following pages: King George VI and Queen Mary visit the blitzed East End.

the Jewish homes of my acquaintance, where the business of hospitality was carried to the ultimate: you were always offered food, and if you dared to decline, a Jewish mother would reel back in astonishment and ask you 'Why not?' As far as I was concerned, family life happened in the kitchen. My memories of the kitchen are that it was warm – even when other rooms of the house were unheated – and it always smelled good. I helped Mum with the cooking, chatted with her and even did my homework on the kitchen table.

Although the East End was once a busy industrial area, the number and range of its industries steadily dwindled. Traditional East End trades had included silk-weaving, the rag trade, metal founding, ship-building and working on the railways or in the docks. The East End was once famous for such firms as the New Canton Works in Bow. This, the first custom-built porcelain factory in Britain, opened on Stratford Causeway, east of Bow Bridge, in 1749. Until its closure in 1776 it made figures and other items and today Bow porcelain is highly collected. The Whitechapel Bell Foundry (32-4 Whitechapel Road, E1) has existed in the area since the sixteenth century and made the bells for Westminster Abbey, Big Ben, the American Liberty Bell and, of course, Bow Bells. Bryant and May's match factory was also a major East End employer. There was a musical called *The Match Girls* – I once performed a song from it. It is concerned with the match girls' strike of 1888. It was the first major strike of women. The work was fraught with hazards, including a dreadful disease called 'Phossy-Jaw' (constant close contact with phosphorous resulted in facial deformity), and they used to get terribly low wages – five to eighteen shillings a week, and women outworkers made match boxes at home for twopence farthing per gross. Writing in 1903, Jack London described this exploitation:

> Conceive an old woman, broken and dying, supporting herself and four children, and paying three shillings per week rent, by making match boxes at 2¼d. per gross. Twelve dozen boxes for 2¼d. and, in addition, finding her own paste and thread! She never knew a day off, either for sickness, rest or recreation. Each day and every day, Sundays as well, she toiled fourteen hours. Her day's stint was seven gross, for which she received 1s. 3¾d. In the week of 98 hours' work she made 7,066 matchboxes, and earned 9s. 2¼d. less paste and thread.

There was a long tradition of casual labour in the East End – especially in the docks. It meant that some men worked when they felt like it, then drank or lazed about when they didn't. Even today, many East Enders prefer the relative freedom of self-employment, and work as window cleaners, fix cars or drive mini-cabs. Taxi-driving among Jewish East Enders was a long-established profession, but these days a good many cab drivers have prospered and moved out to the suburbs, particularly in Essex, such as Ilford, Romford and Gants Hill.

One East End industry that seems to go on from generation to generation is the rag trade. Dad worked in it in the days when it was almost 100 per cent Jewish; now it is largely operated by Bangladeshis – who,

The Whitechapel Bell Foundry, one of the East End's longest-established industries.

Following pages: An old-style rag trade sweatshop and a modern workroom.

like the Jews before them, still run their businesses on a family basis.

One job that at least got East Enders out into the air was hop picking – for years droves of them used to go down to Kent every year for this seasonal occupation. As a schoolboy, Dad went fruit picking in East Anglia. He was paid with metal tokens which could be exchanged in local shops and redeemed at the end of the stint. East Enders took the East End with them, congregating round the fire, eating communally and singing songs. We still do it now!

Left: East End hop-pickers on London Bridge station, before setting off on their annual trip to Kent. Below: Hard at work in the fields.

The Local

The pub in East End social life

C HARLIE Brown, the landlord of the Railway Tavern in West India Dock Road, was called the 'Uncrowned King of Limehouse'. When he died in 1932, his funeral at Tower Hamlets Cemetery was attended by no fewer than 10,000 mourners. That was the sort of esteem in which an East End publican was once held. The pub (at 116 West India Dock Road, E14) was even renamed 'Charlie Brown's'.

What is it that makes an East End pub so special? In television soap operas such as *Coronation Street* – and, of course, *EastEnders*! – the pub is the focal point of activity. This is a commonly-used device for bringing people together so that they can interact – otherwise all the action would be taking place in a series of unrelated little family groups. But in the real East End, the pub always has been genuinely the centre of community life. There are probably more pubs per square mile in the East End than in any other part of the country – and pubs of every size and type, from the smart to the downright sleazy. They are the places where people meet and gossip, where young people gather to make new friends, and where you can observe East Enders at their most relaxed – and sometimes their most boisterous!

Compared with other parts of London, the East End not only has the greatest concentration of pubs serving the 'drinking class', but it has traditionally been well served by its large breweries: for centuries they have been among the major employers in the area – and good employers they were too, famous for the way in which they looked after their employees. In this century, there have been many take-overs and closures. Edward Tilney and Company's Alma Brewery, for example, has gone, though the Alma pub in Spelman Street continues on its site.

The oldest of them is Truman's Black Eagle Brewery at 91 Brick Lane. It was founded in 1666, the year of the Great Fire of London, and once run by Sir Benjamin Truman. By the late nineteenth century, Trumans was the largest brewing company in the world, with stables for 130 dray horses and every ancillary trade from blacksmiths to inn sign painters in its employ. Watney's Albion Brewery at 333-335 Whitechapel Road also expanded enormously in the Victorian period, and is famous for having introduced the first bottled brown ale in England in 1899. Its chairman, Edward Mann, even became the first mayor of Stepney in 1900.

Other local brewers also went in for politics and became notable benefactors of East End charities, but none more so than Frederick Nicholas Charrington. Charrington's Anchor Brewery in Mile End Road had been founded in 1759. Frederick was born in 1850, and was set to run the family business until one day he was passing a public house in the East End when he saw a ragged woman with her children begging her drunken husband for money for food. Realising that it was a Charrington's pub – and racked with guilt – he immediately resolved to improve the life of the poor. He renounced over £1 million-worth of shares, moved to an ordinary house in Stepney and dedicated the rest of his life to raising money for the destitute. Charrington's Brewery continued happily without him, and became a leading East End employer: my first boyfriend worked there, as his father had done before him.

A lot of my earliest recollections, especially our various family gatherings, are associated with East End pubs. Sometimes, at Christmas, after licencing hours, the landlord would close the doors and parties went on as family gatherings. Then members of the family would buy crates of beer and the party would continue back at a relation's home. Men drank pints – bottled beer was always the favourite – brown ale, light ale and stouts such as Mackeson and, in particular, Guinness. Women were especially sold on the adverts that had long been telling them that 'Guinness is Good For You'; they believed it and always remarked on how much good it was doing them! Yet the only occasions I can remember anyone actually getting drunk was in the privacy of our own homes at Christmas. There was drunkenness in the East End – in the nineteenth century the gin palaces and beer shops were prevalent, and many temperance movements attempted to curb the excesses and the effects of alcoholism on people's health and family life. But in modern times it is far less evident, partly I think because most sensible parents encouraged their children to have a healthy respect for drink: instead of making it a 'forbidden fruit', they allowed their children an occasional nip and educated them to the fact that while drink in moderation made you feel good, too much booze made you feel terrible! From an early age I was allowed a little wine or port (an unfashionable drink now, but I still love it!) at family dinners, and although as Den's wife in *EastEnders* I am an alcoholic, this is very far from the real me.

Sundays at East End pubs have always been a special time. I remember how proud I was when my Dad sometimes took me down to

Top: The Karate Club meets at the Queen's Head, Fieldgate Street.

Bottom: Truman's Brewery – a reflection of an East End tradition.

Following pages: East End pub life 40 years ago and today – spot which is which!

our local, the Prince Regent in Globe Road, on Sundays for a pre-dinner drink. Even today, a lot of the pubs have shellfish stalls outside: once they had shellfish and other nibbles free at the bar at Sunday lunchtimes. As Sunday was traditionally the day for visiting relatives, many of the pubs had flower stalls outside, so that you could buy a bunch of daffs for Mum or Auntie.

In my late teens, the Green Gate (228 Bethnal Green Road, E2) became my 'local'. It was the place where young people in the area hung out: wine bars were almost unknown, and discos and dance halls were and still are rare in the East End – one had to go further afield, such as to Ilford or Tottenham: I used to go to hear the Dave Clark Five at the Tottenham Royal, for instance. We experimented with 'trendy' drinks – there were fashions for Campari and soda or for Snowballs (advocaat and lemonade), which we thought highly sophisticated. Girls and fellers dressed up, rather than down, to go pubbing. At this time, young people in the East End polarised between being Mods and Rockers. Today I have a great affection for the 1950s, its clothes and music, but the dirt and grime associated with the Rockers' motorbikes put me right off. While they roared up and down Roman Road on their Triumphs, I gravitated toward the neat, clean Mods on their Lambrettas, and off I went to the bowling alleys and to Southend – freezing to death on the back of a chrome-trimmed scooter! It always seemed

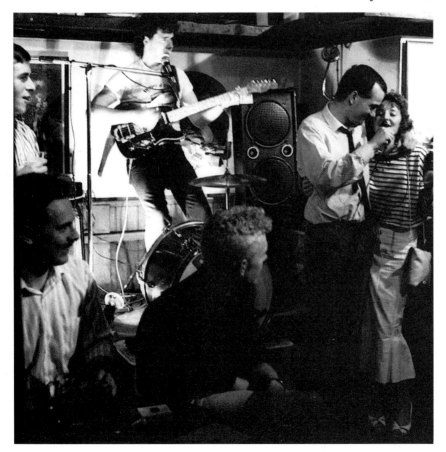

A night out at the Prospect of Whitby.

Landlady Countess Eileen Wolozyska and 'Accordion Andy' at the Queen's Head, Fieldgate Street.

like a great idea at the time, but the actuality never quite lived up to my expectations!

Once I had enrolled in the Webber Douglas Academy in South Kensington, I went for the first time to a South Ken pub and was struck by how different it was from the pubs I used to frequent. I think it was mainly the upper-class accents, and I remember thinking to myself, 'I'll *never* fit in here!' But then I started to pick out the odd regional accent, and began to feel more confident that I was not the only 'outsider' there. I was still living at home. My grant was enough for bare essentials, but no more, so in between terms, in our holiday break, I got a job as a barmaid in the Black Boy (now called Fifth Avenue) in the Mile End Road, not far from where we lived. No sooner had I started work there than my Dad appeared in the pub and ordered a drink. 'What are you doing here?' I asked him. 'I'd like a word with the landlord,' he told me. Calling him over, he told him in concise terms that I was his daughter, and that I was to be treated properly; any problems, and he would be down there to sort things out. After he left, the landlord said to me, 'What a nice bloke! I really respect him for that.' There never were any problems – well, none that were too serious. On one occasion, I had been chatting to a customer, just as good barmaids are supposed to do. After a while, I went to the Ladies, where I was confronted by a tiny East End girl – smaller even than me! – who grabbed me. 'That's my feller!' she snapped, glowering up at me. 'If you don't wanna get a bottle in yer face, you'd better leave off, OK?' 'OK,' I told her. On another occasion, one of the other barmaids, an extremely pretty girl, was similarly doing her professional duty with a customer. Her boyfriend, a gigantic brute, stood nearby, drinking with his friends, watching and fuming. He gave the girl her statutory warning, but the barman

93

intervened, foolishly advising the Incredible Hulk to leave her alone. In one deft movement, the poor barman was hauled over the bar and felled with a single blow.

The pub was a popular venue for young men on their stag nights. Surrounded by his mates, the groom-to-be would be filled with such vast quantities of drink that he ended up legless, and had to be carried home. I always tried to imagine how he might feel the following morning – the most important day of his life – when 'Get me to the church on time' was only half the battle: staying upright and overcoming the effects of the night before was the big challenge.

I can recommend touring some of the East End pubs as a fascinating experience. It enables you to see something of the huge diversity of East End life, and gives you glimpses of the extraordinary history of the area. The dockside is a good place to start: because it was such thirsty work, in the mid-nineteenth century, there were said to be as many as 50 taverns in a single street, St George's Street near St Katharine's Dock. Many of those that have survived have interesting historical associations. The Gun (27 Coldharbour Lane, E14), for instance, was

where Lord Nelson used to meet his mistress, Lady Hamilton. The Grapes (76 Narrow Street, E14) is a wonderful small riverside pub which many people believe is the one Charles Dickens had in mind when he wrote about the 'Six Jolly Fellowship Porters' in *Our Mutual Friend*. 'A bar to soften the human breast . . . not much larger than a hackney-coach' he described it, and it is still immaculately kept, its original wide floorboards and woodwork gleaming and the whole place smelling of rich wax polish. Recently I only just saved myself from going head-over-heels on the shiny floor! I asked the cleaner how often she polished to get it like this. 'Every day,' she told me, apparently surprised that anyone might ask such a daft question, as if to say 'Doesn't *everyone* polish every day?' In the bar there is a painting called 'Saturday Night at the Grapes' by Alice M. West. It was exhibited at the Royal Academy in the year I was born, and shows an East End pub at its best: a warm inviting place, with convivial customers enjoying themselves at their local. Today the Grapes is in an increasingly 'Yuppie' area, in the middle of the Docklands development. Where once you might have had to pick your way through groups of sailors and dockers, you now have to fight to get past the rows of parked Porsches and BMWs!

Also on the river, in Wapping, is the Prospect of Whitby (57 Wapping Wall, E1), which describes itself as 'London's Oldest Riverside Inn'. Dickens was a customer here, but it has an even more ancient history. It was built in 1520, and soon became notorious as a den of thieves and smugglers – hence its original name, the Devil's Tavern. The famous diarist, Samuel Pepys, often visited it – and the Ancient Pepys Society still meets here. For as many years as anyone could remember, a Whitby-registered ship called the *Prospect* was moored nearby, and in 1777 the inn was re-named after it as the 'Prospect of Whitby'. The painters Whistler and Turner often visited the Prospect, and sketched the Thames from its waterfront terrace. It has even had a place in horticultural history: it was here, early in the eighteenth century, that a sailor sold to a local gardener a completely unknown plant he had brought from America. It was the fuchsia.

Also in Wapping is the Town of Ramsgate (62 Wapping High Street, E1). Once called the Red Cow (allegedly after some poor barmaid, who was noted for her red hair!), it has a violent past: there is a story that its garden was once the setting for hangings of pirates and that secret tunnels lead from the pub to the Tower of London. The cellars were certainly used as dungeons for convicts awaiting transportation to Australia. The infamous Lord Chancellor, Judge Jeffreys, 'The Hanging Judge', supported King James II until he fled England in 1688. Jeffreys

Left: The Widow's Son.

Right: An American sailor performs the bun custom in 1982.

attempted to follow, was captured at the pub disguised as a sailor and taken to the Tower, where he died the following year. Nearer to the Tower, the Dickens Inn (St Katharine's Way, E1), though touristy, is another popular old riverside pub.

Mary Kelly, the fifth, last and most horrific victim of Jack the Ripper, used to frequent the Ten Bells pub in Commercial Street. It was later renamed the Jack the Ripper (84 Commercial Street, E1). The Widow's Son (75 Devons Road, E3) was built in 1848 on the site of an unnamed widow's cottage. She was expecting her son home for Easter, and baked him a hot cross bun. He never did return, but she never gave up hope, and every year cooked another bun, which was added to the pile from previous years. The custom has continued until today there are over 200 buns (mostly in the cellar, but about 50 of them still hang in the bar). On Good Friday, a sailor is invited to add another bun to the collection, for which he is rewarded with a pint of beer, and buns are distributed to customers. It was once believed that buns baked on Good Friday never went stale, and had magical powers. In 1982, during the Falklands conflict, there was no British sailor available. This could have been a serious problem, since the landlord's lease is dependant on maintaining the long-standing custom. Fortunately, an acceptable substitute – an American seaman – was found in the nick of time!

There is something for every possible taste in the many hundreds of East End pubs. Hollands (Brayford Square, E1) though only just off the busy Commercial Road, has managed to retain a completely authentic Victorian interior. The Ringside (22 Kingsland Road, E2) run by Vic Andretti, a former lightweight champion contains boxing memorabilia and has a gym upstairs. The Royal Cricketers (211 Old Ford Road, E2) is pleasantly situated alongside the Regent's Canal and is decorated with a collection of cricketing prints; the Palm Tree (24/6 Palm Street, E3) is also on the canal. The Five Bells and Bladebone (27 Three Colt Street, E14) has an appropriate dockland theme, with pictures of tea clippers and docking tools, while the Anchor and Hope (90 Duckett Street, E1) has the unlikely theme of the London Fire Brigade, represented by a collection of their badges. You can even find a haunted East End pub! In 1974 at the Bow Bells (116 Bow Road, E3) there were reports of the ladies' toilet being flushed by an unseen ghostly hand!

If it's live action you're after, many East End pubs offer such games as pool and bar billiards. Darts is especially popular in the East End – City Darts (40 Commercial Street, E1), formerly known as the Princess Alice, actually has a whole pub-full of dartboards, upstairs and down-stairs, as well as live jazz. Live entertainment can also be found at pubs like the Birdcage (80 Columbia Road, E2), which has a talent night, or the Fish and Ring (141A White Horse Road, E1), which won the Best London Pub award in 1985 and which – like many other East End pubs – has a much-used piano. Both live jazz and an Old Tyme Music Hall are available at the Lord Hood (89 Dunbridge Street, E2), and the Crown and Castle (600 Kingsland Road, E8) has a comedy theatre which oper-ates upstairs on Saturdays. The link between pubs and show biz has always been in evidence in the East End: Mary 'Queenie' Watts, former licencee of the Rose and Crown (17 Pennyfields, E14), was a famous jazz singer and actress.

If you can face an early morning drink, you can take advantage of a loophole in our peculiar licensing laws and visit one of the pubs that open in the morning to cater for market traders. The Carpenters Arms (73 Cheshire Street, E2) is open from 8 am to 2 pm on Sundays to serve the habitues of the nearby Club Row pet market, and on weekdays the Golden Heart (110 Commercial St, E1) opens from 6 to 9 am for the Spitalfields Market.

The recently renovated Blind Beggar (337 Whitechapel Road, E1) gained notoriety when on 6 March 1966 Ronnie Kray and an accom-plice murdered George Cornell as he sat drinking there. The pub's atmosphere has changed dramatically now, and with a pleasant gar-den for children, it has become, like so many other East End pubs, a place for the entire family.

The Blind Beggar – once the scene of gangland violence, now a popular family pub.

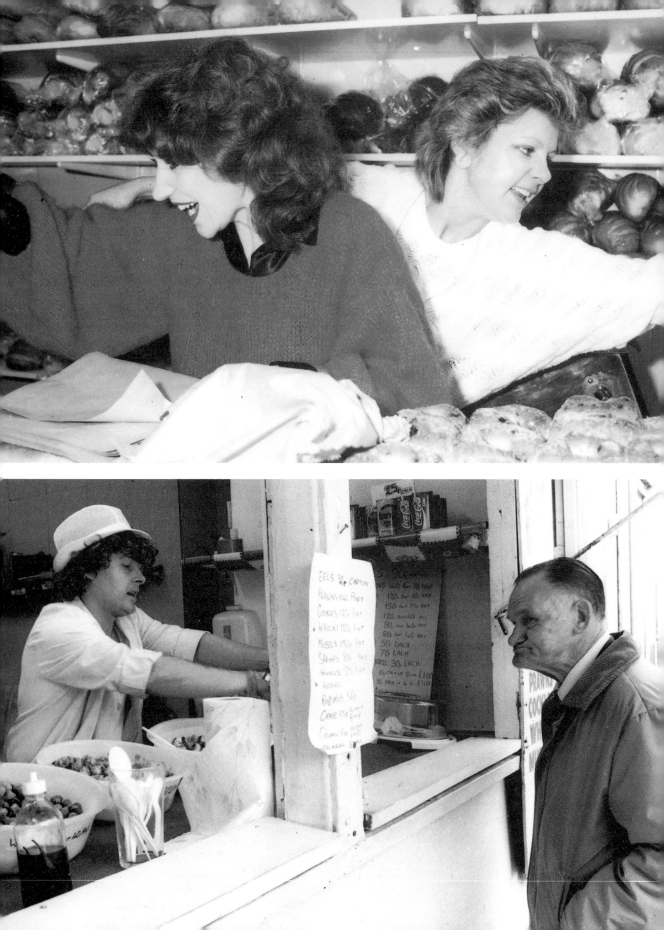

Lovely Grub

The East Ender's traditional fare

STAGE comedians who want to depict a 'typical' Cockney have only to dress up in a pearly king's outfit and sing a line or two of 'Boiled Beef and Carrots'. The song was made popular in the days of the music halls by Harry Champion, who built his career on such celebrations of Londoners' eating habits: 'Next to drinking, of course, the Londoner loves eating,' wrote Thomas Burke in his 1915 book, *Nights on the Town*. 'Mr Harry Champion, with the insight of a genius, has divined this, and therefore he sings about food. . .' (One of his other food songs was actually called 'Baked Sheep's Heart Stuffed with Sage and Onions'!) A lot of Cockney slang has to do with food. Not only was it obviously a preoccupation of people who didn't have much, but in a deprived society treats of any kind meant a great deal. 'Earning a crust' and remarking that someone has more of something 'than I've had hot dinners' are just two of many Cockney expressions that relate to grub.

East Enders, in particular, have always been 'partial' to certain traditional dishes. Over 60 years ago, in his book, *Blind Man's Buff*, Louis Hemon described how a visitor to Petticoat Lane market would find 'quiet corners in which he may solace himself with a plate of green peas or a portion of eel in jelly.' Things haven't changed too much: the East End is still a part of the country where people have clung to their favourite foods, and the two that Hemon mentions are still popular. The 'green peas' sold by street traders was pease pudding. It was once widely eaten in Britain, but has always been especially popular among Cockneys, and was even described by one writer as 'the immortal pease pudding'. I have eaten it, usually with saveloys – a kind of spicy sausage. 'Pease pudding and saveloys' is mentioned as one of the delectable meals Oliver Twist dreams about in the song, 'Food, Glorious Food' from Lionel Bart's *Oliver!*. It's also the subject of the well-

known nursery rhyme that goes:

> Pease pudding hot, pease pudding cold,
> Pease pudding in the pot, nine days old.

If you fancy trying it out, there's an old recipe for it in a nineteenth-century cookery book called *The Cook's Oracle* by Dr William Kitchener:

> Put a quart of split peas into a clean cloth; do not tie them up too close, but leave a little room for them to swell; put them on to boil in cold water slowly until they are tender; if they are good peas they will be boiled enough in about two hours and a half; rub them through a sieve into a deep dish, and add an egg or two, an ounce of butter, and some pepper and salt; beat them well together for about ten minutes [or about ten seconds in a food blender!], until these ingredients are well incorporated; then flour the cloth well, put the pudding in, tie up as tight as possible, and boil it an hour longer. It is as good with boiled beef as it is with boiled pork.

The other characteristic East End dish is eels. Many people – and I have to confess, I am among them! – have an aversion to live eels, probably because they think of them as a kind of water snake. But in fact they are very good to eat; they are said to contain 20 per cent more protein than steak, and only 25 per cent of the fat of red meat. Jellied eels are the best-known Cockney dish. The eels are chopped up, boiled, drained and set in aspic jelly. Eel pie is a complete meal, and all over the East End you can still find the traditional 'eel and pie shops'. Despite their name, they are often more than 'shops', and usually have seating for customers to eat on the premises as well as a take-away counter. At Saturday lunchtimes there are often big queues. Frederick Cooke (41 Kingsland High Street, E8) is one of the most famous. The firm has been in business since 1862 and still retains its original decor, with a restaurant and take-away service for jellied eels and pie and mash, served with a 'liquor' of green parsley sauce. They have always been sold live – hence the old East End street traders' cry of 'Live eels!' – because they are more digestible if they are killed and skinned immediately before cooking. Unfortunately, this means you have to bash the eel on the head! If you can face it, Mrs Beeton's Victorian recipe for eel pie is as close as you can get to the authentic East End dish:

> Ingredients:
> 1½ lbs eels
> ½ pint meat stock
> 1 tablespoonful of mushroom ketchup
> 1 desertspoonful of lemon juice
> Pepper, salt, puff pastry

Method:
Clean and skin the eels, and cut them into pieces about two inches

Preceding page and above: Frederick Cooke's, one of the East End's most famous eel and pie shops.

long. Put the heads, tails and fins in a stewpot with the stock, simmer for about half an hour, then strain, and skim well. Place the eels in a pie dish with a good seasoning of salt and pepper between the layers. Add the lemon juice and ketchup to the stock, pour about half of it into the pie dish, cover with paste, and bake in a fairly hot oven for about one hour. Warm the remainder of the stock, and pour it into the pie through a funnel as soon as it is cooked.

Sufficient for five persons.

The cafe has steadily replaced the traditional East End street trader.

Here's another secret – please don't tell anyone, but I don't like shell-fish either! As I come from the East End, you might assume I would like nothing better than a plate of whelks or cockles – perhaps, in view of my character in *EastEnders*, washed down with a glass or six of gin. In fact, I hate gin! I once had to do a personal appearance, and the organisers were set up by so-called 'friends' to lay on a spread featuring – you've guessed it – whelks and gin! The organisers were so kind and only trying to please me, but my stomach turned at the sight. Fortunately, the ever hungry and thirsty Press helped out and wolfed down the lot. But most East Enders are not as fussy as me and they simply adore shellfish – many East End pubs have shellfish stalls outside, selling mussels, whelks and cockles as well as crabs and other more exotic items. Tubby Isaacs' shellfish stall in Petticoat Lane market has been there so long it is part of the scenery. Shrimps and winkles were once the usual fare for an East End Sunday tea. Winkles (the Cockney name for periwinkles) are boiled in salty water for twenty minutes and 'winkled' out of their shells with pins, to be dipped in vinegar and eaten with slices of bread and butter. East Enders have always eaten them – especially on their outings to Southend – much to the astonishment of outsiders, who can't understand why anyone should go to so much trouble for such a tiny morsel of food. Writing in the 1940s, Augusta Arnold, an American marine biologist, noted with snobbish amazement that 'in Great Britain they are used among the poorer classes for food'!

The East End once supported numerous street food traders, like the muffin men, hot potato and pie sellers, but these had all disappeared from the streets before I was born.

However, we still had a man who came round with a tray of toffee apples on his bicycle, and I could never resist them! If you aren't lucky enough to have a friendly neighbourhood toffee apple seller, you can make your own: mix ½ lb treacle (molasses), 1 lb brown sugar and 1 tablespoon of vinegar and boil it for 20-30 minutes. Impale ripe apples on sticks and dip them in the mixture, laying them to set on a flat surface with the stick upright. The toffee runs down and you get that wonderful hard flattened mass of toffee on the top of the apple! Mind your teeth!

Fish and chips is the other eternally popular dish. When Dad was a boy, it was twopence for fish and a penny for chips, so a family of four could be well fed for a shilling. The East End can't claim any monopoly on it, but I remember it as a popular meal of my childhood. Friday evenings were 'fish and chip night', and you can still see the queues on Fridays outside every East End chip shop. It was always served in newspaper with lashings of salt and vinegar. One of the best East End fish and chip shops is the Sea Shell (424-426 Kingsland Road, E8) which sells over the counter as well as having a busy restaurant.

As a child, I recall rabbit stew was always very popular – with everyone, that is, except me. As mentioned earlier, I loved rabbits, and once I discovered what I was eating, refused to touch it. I loved (and still love) bacon sandwiches, but the other end of the pig – its trotters or 'pettitoes' – once very popular in the East End, was not on my list of favourites. I adored Mum's good home cooking – her shepherd's pies, stews with dumplings, toad-in-the-hole, steak and kidney puddings and of course the Sunday roast. Her desserts were out of this world – especially her apple pie, treacle pudding and bread pudding.

I realise now what none of us was really conscious of until we started travelling abroad and going out to restaurants, and that is just how very English our diet was. Now I've read more about cookery and the history of the East End, it's more obvious to me that, until relatively recently, what we ate was not much different from the sort of food that was eaten a hundred years ago: only now we've been introduced to fast food, to hamburgers, pizzas, kebabs and other foreign foods, do we start to recall and appreciate the forgotten flavours of our food heritage.

Should the fancy take you, it's still perfectly possible to eat good English food in the East End. St Katharine's Dock – one of my favourite spots in the whole area – has the Dickens Inn (St Katharine's Way, E1) which contains no fewer than three restaurants in a former warehouse, and Nick's Place (137 Leman Street, E1) also serves good, traditional food. Steak houses can be found all over the East End – for example La Bohème (564 Mile End Road, E3) and the Venus Steak House (368 Bethnal Green Road, E2).

The East End always has been and still is strong on cafés – or 'caffs' as we always call them – serving good value meals of the 'greasy spoon' variety: fried eggs, bacon, sausages, beans and chips, great doorsteps of bread and large cups of tea: great for dockers and others with good appetites and no worries about their cholesterol levels!

As the East End has long been a sort of ethnic melting-pot, it has drawn in foods from all round the world. In fact, a lot of its supposedly 'traditional' foods probably filtered in from other parts of the country and overseas, such as from Ireland, when the navvies moved in during the nineteenth century. Another wave of immigrants, the Jews, brought in a further extension to the East End culinary repertoire. The irresistible aroma of bread from the Jewish bakeries is one of my abiding memories of going shopping in the East End, and it must be one of the few places in the country with an all-night bagel (or beigel) bakery, in Brick Lane, which sells bagels with every known filling. If you don't have a bagel baker near you, you can make your own:

1 lb plain flour
2 oz butter
½ pt milk
1 oz sugar
1 eggyolk
1 teaspoon salt
1 oz yeast

Mix and leave to rise in warm place, drop in boiling water; they sink to the bottom, and rise when cooked; take out and sprinkle with poppy or caraway seeds, bake until golden brown, spread with cream cheese – or any other filling you fancy.

Behind the scenes in a bagel bakery.

Blooms (90 Whitechapel High Street, E1) is one of London's most famous Jewish restaurants. They have a take-away counter, too, that always does a roaring trade, and it's well worth queuing for their salt beef.

The Chinese influence in Limehouse wasn't all opium dens: they introduced their own cuisine, and to this day some of London's best Chinese restaurants can be found in an otherwise bleak part of dock-lands, among them Good Friends (139 Salmon Lane, E14), New Friends (53 West India Dock Road, E14), Young Friends (11 Pennyfields, E14) and Chinatown (795 Commercial Road, E14).

The East End has Britain's largest Bangladeshi community, so it's not surprising to find a cluster of Indian restaurants, mostly around Brick Lane, such as the Clifton (126 Brick Lane, E1) or Al Madina (166 Brick Lane) which stays open until 2.30 am. The Star Bhel Poori House (17 New Road, E1) serves some unusual Indian dishes and is very popular with students from the nearby London Hospital.

The East End continues its long cosmopolitan tradition: you can get West Indian food at BG's Restaurant (542 Kingsland Road, E8) and even vegetarian Buddhist at the Cherry Orchard (241-245 Globe Road, E2), and you can eat Italian beside Regent's Canal at Lower East Side (230 Old Ford Road, E2). From the outside, it looks unimpressive, but inside it's cosy and charming, and has the unexpected feature of a gangplank leading over the canal to a secluded bar.

Following pages: One of the East End's many Indian restaurants.

109

Down The Market

Shopping East End style

EAST Enders love trying to make a fast buck, and they simply adore finding a bargain. The numerous East End markets are the places where you can see both of these in action. There are general markets that sell everything and anything – clothes, fruit, vegetables and hardware, the sort of things you can probably buy more easily and more cheaply in any supermarket, but East End markets are far more fun than any supermarket! Everything is out on display to be extolled by the patter of the stallholders – all of them attempting to catch the eye and ear and persuading you to buy – even things you don't really need. Often the trader may have a regular pitch, though many of them move to other locations on different days of the week. As a child, I was fascinated by the East End markets. They seemed to be designed for children, and many of the stalls had treats for kids such as toys – furry, whirring, prancing things – sweets, junk jewellery, charms (I still have one of a little bird bought for me by Bill, my grandfather, when I was very tiny), bracelets, earrings, necklaces, as well as things like brightly-coloured shoes, mittens, purses and handbags (I seemed to collect them, though how many handbags does a child actually need?!). We used to stop for freshly-baked doughnuts – the ones with the jam that squirted out when you bit into them – and buns covered with icing.

Until recently, I often went to East End markets to pick up odds and ends, such as flowers for Mum. Now, since the success of *EastEnders*, it's not so easy. It's great that everyone enjoys the programme so much, but as you can imagine, if I stop to talk to one person, I'd want to do it with everyone! My days of taking a leisurely stroll through an East End market seem today to be few and far between.

Petticoat Lane is not only the most famous East End market, in fact,

it is probably the most famous of all London markets. Every year millions of Londoners and tourists flock on Sunday mornings to its thousand or more stalls. It is hard to imagine amid all the bustle that, as one earlier writer described, 'both sides of Petticoat Lane were hedgerows and elm trees with pleasant fields to walk in, insomuch that some gentlemen of the Court and City built their houses here for air.'

Petticoat Lane's connection with clothing has a long tradition. First the Huguenot weavers, and then the Jewish traders sold clothes here – hence its name. It was called Hog Lane before, and officially changed to Middlesex Street in 1830, but 'Petticoat Lane' has stuck. Its sheer number of stalls and variety of items for sale has always struck visitors. Daniel Kirwan, an American traveller in London, wrote in 1870 about the part of the market in Clothier and Cutler Streets, describing the '. . .hundreds and hundreds of pairs of trousers, thousands of spencers [a type of coat], high-lows [boots], fustian jackets, some greasy, some unsoiled, shooting-coats, short coats, and cutaways: drawers and stockings, the latter washed and hung up in all their appealing innocence. Milling around were two hundred men, women and children mostly of the Jewish race and here and there a burly Irishman sitting smoking a pipe amid the infernal din.'

Preceding pages: A bustling East End livestock market.

Opposite: The shop that sells everything! Bow, 1936.
Below: Bikes for sale in Brick Lane Market.

Today Petticoat Lane still predominantly sells cheap clothing. A short walk from it will take you to Brick Lane and the adjoining streets – another Sunday morning market, which has a much more general range of goods, including a fine selection of junk!

Whitechapel Market (which extends on Saturdays to take in the Mile End Waste) operates every day *except* Sunday. Before regulations changed, it was open in the evenings and must have presented quite a spectacle. A visitor to it one evening in 1901 described it vividly:

There are fruit and vegetable stalls, there are fish stalls, haberdashers, stationers', tailors, toy, jewellery, butchers', cutlery, boot, hat and cap, and unmistakeably second-hand ironmongery stalls, all along to Mile End Gate; and, to add to the crush and the tumult, enterprising shopkeepers have rushed selections of their goods out of doors and ranged them among the stalls and set assistants bawling in wildernesses of furniture and crockery, or chanting incessantly amidst clustered pillars of linoleum and carpet like lay priests in ruined temples.

The stalls and those overflowings of the shops are intersected by stands where weary marketers may solace themselves with light refreshment in the way of whelks liberally seasoned with vinegar and pepper, cheap but indigestible pastry, toffee apples; and there are ice-cream barrows that dispense ices and ginger-beer in summer and in winter supply baked potatoes and hot drinks.

Intersecting other stalls are a cripple in a wheeled-chair manipulating a concertina; a man with a tray suspended round his neck selling 'electric' pens; an enormous brass weighing machine that soars up glittering and catching light from all the surrounding naptha lamps till it seems itself a thing of fire; a galvanic battery and a 'lung-tester', both popular with boys, who take shocks from the one and blow into the long tube of the other with a joy in the results that is worth at least twice what they pay for it; and, with a naptha lamp all to himself, a sombre, wooden-legged man presides over a seedy collection of umbrellas stuck in a rickety home-made stand and holds a specimen umbrella open over his head as if he lived at the best of times in an invisible shower.

Today, Whitechapel market is not quite so colourful, but it is still worth a visit. My Dad has been going there for years to buy books from Jim Wolveridge's book stall. Mr Wolveridge is himself the author of *Ain't It Grand*, an entertaining account of life in Stepney in the 1930s, and co-author, with Robert Barltrop, of a fascinating survey of the Cockney language, *The Muvver Tongue*.

There are a number of other general street markets around the East End, each serving its local community: this was especially important in the days when no-one had a car, so all shopping had to be done as close to home as possible. They include Bethnal Green Road, Watney

The Columbia Market – a popular source of cut-price plants.

Following pages: Some typical East End market scenes.

market (off Commercial Road), Chrisp Street (a modern, functional market on the Lansbury Estate, Poplar), and Ridley Road. Roman Road has a large market, mainly clothes, and Columbia Road a nice Sunday morning flower and plant market. On Saturdays only, Kingsland Waste has a market specialising in tools, do-it-yourself materials and all sorts of odd bits and pieces that you'd never find anywhere else.

The East End also boasts a couple of important wholesale markets: Billingsgate, the famous fish market, was in the City of London until 1982, when it was re-sited on the Isle of Dogs. The redevelopment of more than 11 acres of Spitalfields fruit, vegetable and flower market is also planned – a £200 million enterprise involving the building of offices, homes and shops and relocating the market. The City of London owns the site, which has been offered for sale for a sum in excess of £70 million!

I ought to explain here about a group of people that everyone thinks of as quintessentially Cockney – the pearly kings and queens. They have always been associated with the London markets' fruit and veget-able organisation – and that has been their main function ever since. amazing costumes covered with thousands of pearl buttons. Firstly, many people think that they have been around for hundreds of years and, secondly, that they come from the East End. Neither is true. They were more or less invented about a century ago by Henry Croft, who died on New Year's Day, 1930. He was a road sweeper who worked in Covent Garden market. As he was an orphan, he was determined to do something to help other orphans, and created the 'Pearlies' as a charit-able organization – and that has been their main function ever since. There is no sex-discrimination and they inherit through both male and female lines, chosing an area for themselves as their 'kingdom'. It might be an East End locale, but it's just as likely to be in North or South London – or even, nowadays, somewhere like Stevenage!

East End shops are as varied as you could hope to find anywhere – though there are hardly any really large stores. I miss Gardiners, the big shop that long stood in Whitechapel: people used to arrange to meet each other at 'Gardiner's Corner'. It was demolished as part of a road-widening scheme. The East End also had London's first ever Co-op, established in Leman Street in 1879. Between the wars, East End shops were still capable of exciting visitors. Thomas Burke, writing in 1932, wrote an exceptionally graphic description:

In the small territory of the East End are shops as fascinating as any I have found in the dozen cities of Europe that I happen to know. You have not only shops for all the things you may buy in other parts of London, including platinum, genuine pearls and diamonds, furs of sable and seal, exclusive perfumes, and pâté de fois gras; but shops for things that can be bought in few other places, such as sheep bells and church bells, areca nut and shark's fins. Here you can buy interesting pastries, and sweets that are never seen in the 'better' shops – toffee-apples, humbugs, brandy snaps, pop-corn, sherbet, colt's foot, locusts, and surprise packets. Without moving out of a particular street you can buy

Roumanian beads, pelts, Dutch drops, nautical charts, praying-shawls, costers' barrows, freshcut chaff from the hay-market, milk fresh from the cow, flags and bunting and pilots' manuals. . . . There are shops for all manner of half-forgotten herbs – pennyroyal, saffron, tansy, senna and rue. There is a shop where you can buy your whitebait wholesale. There are shops for mystic emblems of strange faiths. And there is a shop where you can buy things I have sought vainly in West End shops; namely, all the world's gramophone records. Records of music and songs and stories and lamentations and warcries made by the peoples of China, Persia, Armenia, Syria, Arabia, Egypt, West Africa, Turkey, Roumania, Russia, Greece and Korea, and the various provinces of India. At the Docks you may buy an 'odd lot' of such delightfully mixed matters as lithophone, ochre, Hanchow bags, petits pois, tapioca, gum copal, slag, graphite, chicory and spelter; though what you would do with such a lot when you got it home I don't know. Give it to an artist friend, I think, for a study in still-life. There are, in the side-streets off other side-streets, shops which are not shops at all, but merely, as in country villages, cottages which have turned their front-parlours into shops and their parlour windows into public spectacles and rendezvous for the children. There are shops which, besides being tobacconists' or hairdressers' or tea-shops, also sell hot and cold baths. But most exciting of all are the odds-and-ends shops.

These are not the shops of the curio-dealers or rag-and-bone men. They are shops whose stock is new but of such an insanely assorted kind that fifty guesses would not help you to name in a phrase their owners' line of business, unless you compromised on the word *Everything*. Indeed, at sight of them it seems that anything that cannot be got elsewhere could be got in these shops – if the owner were able to find it.'

I have worked in a couple of East End shops, but none so exotic as any of these. While I was at school, I had a Saturday morning job in Percy Ingle's bakery in Hackney High Road, and worked in Woolworths, Aldgate (the shop is no longer there). You mustn't laugh when I reveal that I worked on the men's underwear counter! I also served on the makeup and other counters, but I repeatedly seemed to be sent back into men's vests and pants. It was a job filled with incident (well, let's be truthful – a couple of incidents!) Once a boy came into the shop when I was temporarily out of underwear and behind the Christmas card counter. He selected some cards, but instead of handing over the money, gave me a handful of maggots, which he and his mates thought was a big joke. I wonder where he is now? I also wonder about the young man who came into the shop regularly every Saturday, and asked me to marry him. When a new girl started, he still came in – and proposed to us both! Perhaps he was jailed for bigamy.

Preceding pages: Pearly kings and queens with their MP, Frank Briant, 1932. Opposite: Some things never change! Kids buying everything in sight.

Rabbit And Pork

Daisy roots, plates of meat, Irish jig, boat race, mince pies, rabbit, rabbit, rabbit . . .

Cockneys and their language

AS I HAVE already mentioned, a Cockney is a person born within the sound of Bow Bells – but even if one could hear the bells, does it mean that anyone born in the City or East End is automatically a Cockney – and what is a Cockney when he or she's at home anyway?

Firstly, what does the word 'Cockney' mean? There are lots of theories as to its origin, several of them pretty daft! Some have said it's because they are cocky; others tell a story about how an ignorant town-dweller who went to the country and heard a cock crowing remarked that the 'cock neighs'! Another version is that it's from a French word *acoquiné*, meaning 'a villain'. Strange though it may seem, however, the probable origin is from 'cokeney', a word that originally meant a 'cock's egg'. Of course, in nature this is an impossibility, but it was once the confusing term given to a small mis-shapen egg; then, in the odd way in which words change their meaning, it came to be used to describe a spoilt or foolish child – 600 years ago, Chaucer used 'Cockney' to mean 'a fool'; then Shakespeare used it in *King Lear* to mean a squeamish woman! Country-dwellers came to use it to refer to townspeople, and the ordinary Londoner was, to any outsider, a 'Cockney'. In the nineteenth century, a Cockney was defined as 'an

uneducated native of London . . . pert and conceited, yet truly ignorant.' It was used as a term of derision, and poets such as John Keats
were looked down on as members of the 'Cockney School' of poetry.

While other regional accents are regarded as interesting, culturally
important or otherwise socially acceptable, Cockney is often frowned
upon as 'bad' English. On the other hand, many observers have recognised the strengths of the Cockney-speaker:

> He is often witty; he is sometimes eloquent; he has a notable gift
> of phrase-making and nicknaming. Every day he is enriching the
> English tongue with new forms of speech, new clichés, new slang,
> new catch-words. The new thing and the new word to describe
> the new thing are never very far apart in London.

Edwin Pugh, *Harry the Cockney*, 1912

How did the Cockney language come about? 'London English' the
variety of English used at court and among wealthy merchants – developed into 'Standard English', what, in its most refined form, we now
call 'BBC English'. Cockney was a dialect – the language of the working
class. They were steadily pushed out of the City of London, where
Standard English ruled, into the East End; then immigrants from other
parts of Britain and overseas came in, bringing new words.

This process has continued into this century, with British soldiers
serving overseas bringing back foreign words which we have incor-
porated into Cockney.

The language is like the East End itself: just as the East End has
absorbed new immigrant communities and has responded to changing
fortunes, Cockney seems to have been able to absorb all these new
influences, to have created and cast aside words and phrases as and
when it felt the need. The result is a hotchpotch version of English that
everyone recognises and which has spilt over into the English of other
parts of Britain and even to foreign countries.

The caricature of the Cockney is unmistakeable. They all wear cloth
caps and mufflers (when they aren't in their pearly king outfits), and
are always eating jellied eels. They use colourful phrases like 'lor luv a
duck!' and call everyone 'guv'nor'. My Dad's generation had the worst
kind of bogus Cockney inflicted on them in films of the 'thirties. In most
stereotyped images there is often some element of truth. Some Germans may wear *lederhosen* and sing drinking songs, some Frenchmen
may wear striped jerseys and berets, and I suppose the odd Australian
has worn a hat with corks dangling from it. But most of them don't –
and it's the same with us Cockneys. Some may fit into the caricature,
but most don't. In particular, any Cockney who spoke continually in
rhyming slang would be regarded by his friends as off his rocker!

My parents and I have lived in the East End pretty much all our lives,
and there are lots of supposedly widely-used rhyming slang words that
we have not only never used, but never even heard anyone else use.
We would be as mystified as anyone if someone asked us to pass the
'army and navy' when they wanted gravy, or if a bus inspector asked to
see our 'bat and wicket' rather than ticket.

Lor luv a duck

The title of this chapter is an example of rhyming slang. Why 'rabbit and pork'? Pork rhymes with 'talk', but in the odd way rhyming slang works, it isn't enough to choose a word that simply rhymes – it has to be part of a phrase; where it becomes *really* confusing to outsiders is when the part of the phrase that actually rhymes is dropped, and the word that doesn't rhyme is used on its own – so we say 'rabbit' (remember the Chas and Dave song, 'Rabbit'?), and say of a talkative person that they are 'rabbiting on'. Dropping the second word is not universal, however: we say that something 'pen and inks' (stinks), but never that it 'pens'!

Experts have been arguing for years about why rhyming slang was invented. The only thing they agree on – more or less! – is that it started in the East End early in the last century. Some say it was the secret language of thieves and beggars. Some think portions of it came over with the Irish navvies – while others reckon it was invented by Cockneys specifically so their rival Irish dock workers wouldn't be able to understand them! Perhaps it came from the jargon of street traders – or maybe it was a spontaneous, humorous way of jazzing up everyday speech, with Cockney wits coming up with more and more bizarre and roundabout ways of saying quite mundane things.

Some rhyming slang is certainly pretty obscure: some words are the names of long-forgotten people, such as 'Kate Carney' (army), after a

popular 1890s music hall comedienne. Some words also depend on the way in which a native Cockney speaker pronounces them: 'the old joanna' seems an odd rhyme for piano unless you know that Cockneys pronounce it 'pianna'.

Most parts of the body acquired rhyming slang names: your face is your 'boat race', your hair is called your 'barnet' (from Barnet Fair), and your eyes 'minces' or 'mincers' (from mince pies). The feet are always 'plates of meat' and the mouth is the 'north and south' – I remember Tommy Steele singing *'What a mouth, what a mouth, what a north and south, blimey what a mouth he's got.'* My Dad recalls hands being customarily called 'Germans' (from German bands), and a wig was usually an 'Irish jig'. If someone was deaf, they are said to be 'Mutt and Jeff', after the American cartoon characters. Rhyming slang also provided roundabout ways of saying what many Cockneys would otherwise have been too embarrassed to say, so there are many rhyming slang words for intimate parts of the anatomy.

Various items of clothing have rhyming slang terms: a hat is always a 'titfer' (from tit-for-tat), a suit is a 'whistle and flute' – usually abbreviated to 'whistle', although a 'dicky dirt' (shirt) is never shortened to 'dicky', since this means ill (from 'Uncle Dick', sick). Trousers are 'round the houses' and a pocket a 'Lucy Lockett'; a tie is sometimes called a 'Peckham Rye', socks 'almond rocks' or 'almonds' and I remember Bill, my grandfather, calling his boots his 'daisies' (from daisy roots): in the Lonnie Donegan song, 'My Old Man's a Dustman', there is the line *he has such a job to pull 'em on, he calls 'em 'daisy roots.* And as an example of how rhyming slang is being continuously invented, a few years ago 'Alan Whickers' came into use for knickers!

A lot of rhyming slang came from other obvious Cockney preoccupations – money (or lack of it), the home, family and problems of one sort or another. Anyone who is really hard up is always described as being 'boracic' (from boracic lint, skint). In my Dad's youth, if you were poor you were said to be 'on the floor', and wages were called 'greengages'. Supper is 'Tommy Tucker' (from the nursery rhyme, 'Little Tommy Tucker sang for his supper' – and hence the Australian word 'tucker', for food in general). Parts of the house were named: the stairs are 'apples and pears', the table is 'Cain and Abel', a cupboard a 'Mother Hubbard' and – before my time – a clock was a 'dickory dock'. A husband might have a 'bull and a cow' (row) with his 'trouble and strife' (wife) who would perhaps get 'in a two and eight' (a state). If a 'tealeaf' (thief) were to 'half-inch' (pinch) something, he might find himself doing 'bird' (bird lime, time – a jail sentence).

Some rhyming slang words have become extremely widely used: most people today would understand what was meant by 'having a butchers' (even if they didn't realise it came from 'butcher's hook', a

look), or they might ask, 'would you Adam and Eve it?' – Eve rhyming
with believe. Everyone knows the expression 'getting down to brass
tacks', but few know it comes from rhyming slang for facts. To 'earwig'
something is to understand it, from the rhyme with twig; 'dustbin lids'
are kids and a 'jam jar' a car. Being 'on your Jack' or 'on your Tod' both
mean on your own – from Jack Jones and Tod Sloan (a famous jockey).
When the weather is cold, people often say 'its's taters!', but until recently I didn't know why. I found out that it comes from 'taters in the
mould' (that is, in the ground), cold.

Rhyming slang changes from generation to generation. There are a
number of terms I have never been inclined to use – but which my Dad
used: 'Johnny Horner' (corner), 'ball of chalk' (walk), 'Bo-Peep'
(sleep), 'Cherry Hogg' (dog), 'dig in the grave' (shave), 'linen draper'
(paper), and so on. Rhyming slang has not only changed and evolved,
particularly in the East End, but it has also been exported to Australia
and the USA for 100 years or more: many words and phrases are either
identical or very similar to their East End roots. It has also been spread
all over Britain in recent years in a variety of ways: a number of terms
for the numbers called out in bingo halls are rhyming slang – 'me and
you' – two; 'door to door' – four; 'cock and hen' – ten; 'clickety-click' –

sixty-six, and so on. But the greatest influence has undoubtedly been that of television. TV comedies have not only given rhyming slang a wide audience, but they have also been responsible for inventing some words and phrases. Galton and Simpson's scripts for *Steptoe and Son* were full of colourful rhyming slang; it is said that the now widespread use of 'Brahms and Liszt' (pissed) derives from its use on the programme, as it was apparently rarely used before. Similarly characters such as Alf Garnett in Johnny Speight's *Till Death Us Do Part*, Ronnie Barker in *Porridge*, who used such terms as 'flowery dell' (cell), and Arthur Daley, who in *Minder* gave us 'her indoors', have helped keep rhyming slang alive – if it ever showed signs of dying! One programme was even named after a rhyming slang term – 'Sweeney', from Sweeney Todd, slang for flying squad.

There are, of course, many Cockney words that are not derived from rhyming slang, and which are no longer used exclusively by Cockneys: a number of words derived from the inevitable 'spots of bother' that occurred – a 'palaver' or a 'ding-dong' (an argument) might develop into a 'shindy' (a fight) in which people would use their 'maulers' or 'mitts' (hands) or put up their 'dukes' (fists). People are said to be 'mogadored' (stumped); they can be 'lairy' (gaudy) or have a 'knees-up' (a party). Some Cockney usages involve a certain amount of exaggeration – for example saying one is 'choked' (annoyed), or that something is 'diabolical' or 'chronic' (unpleasant) or 'a blinder' (a success).

Many writers have attempted to present the Cockney language not only in the variety of its words and phrases, but also in its accent: Charles Dickens and George Bernard Shaw were two exponents who succeeded with varying degrees of accuracy. Many people have argued about whether a real Cockney Eliza Dolittle in *Pygmalion* – better known as the stage and film musical, *My Fair Lady* – would ever have said some of the things Shaw had her say. Some authors have even attempted to write entire stories or poems in phonetic Cockney.

Terms such as 'you're a scholar and a gent' and 'she's a real lady' are widely used by Cockneys, who are renowned for their politeness. There are many Cockney forms of address, ranging from the classic 'me old china' (from rhyming slang – 'china plate', mate) to 'mush'. There are all sorts of subtle ways in which they are used: you might, for instance, say, 'Now look here, chum', as a polite warning, but you would never say, 'Look here, chief'. 'Chief', like 'squire', 'guv'nor' or 'gaffer' always has a suggestion of the person you are speaking to being slightly superior – a tradesman's customer, for example – even though such terms are often also used in a joking way. Calling someone 'mate' or 'my old mate' is perhaps the most usual form, along with 'cock', 'dear', 'duck', 'John' or 'love'. A man will often refer to his wife as 'my old lady' – or 'old girl' to her face – and she will call her husband 'the old man'. There are also numerous conventional Cockney responses to any form of greeting: the simple 'How are you?' will be answered with anything from 'Can't complain' to 'Mustn't grumble' – and there are plenty of Cockneys who, if you ask them how they are, will proceed to tell you in quite some detail!

Cockney has always been good not only at inventing new ways of saying things, but also borrowing words and phrases from elsewhere: to 'take a dekko', to look, was originally a gypsy word – Cockneys presumably heard gypsy street traders urging them to 'take a dekko' at something they were selling. To 'take a shufti', meaning more or less the same, is an Arabic word, brought back by British soldiers serving overseas. Along with sailors entering the East End docks, they brought back all manner of words that quickly became part of everyday speech, spreading out beyond Cockney into everyday English: 'char', tea, originated in China; 'akkas' or 'ackers', money, came from the word for an Egyptian coin, and 'buckshee', free, from the Indian, *baksheesh*, a tip. Euphemisms came from the same sources: for example 'Khyber Pass', rhyming slang for arse. One of my favourites is to to say that someone has gone 'doolally tap', meaning they are crazy. This is pure Indian: Deolali was a town in India with a hospital to which soldiers were sent when they had *tap*, a fever.

In view of the once large Jewish population in the East End, it is not surprising that a lot of words used by Cockneys came from Yiddish, many of them relating to trade, especially the rag trade – words like 'schmutter' or 'clobber', clothing, 'mazuma' or 'gelt', money, 'in stook', in financial difficulties. 'Gezump', to swindle, is now widely used as the term 'gazump', to make a higher offer on a house after a lower one has been accepted. A 'shemozzle' is a row or confusion; we might wish someone 'muzeltov' – good luck; a 'tukas' or 'tokhis' is the backside.

For outsiders, the only way to begin to understand Cockney is to listen to it in use in the East End – an experience not to be missed!

East End
Entertainment

The East End's theatrical, sporting and artistic tradition

I THINK I always knew I wanted to be a professional actress. As well as my joy in acting when I was at school, my Dad was always keen on Shakespeare, and talked to me about his favourite speeches, and I remember when I was very young being taken to the 1953 film of *Julius Caesar* with James Mason as Brutus, and thinking how wonderful he was. I was also keen on classic black and white films – actors like Bette Davis and Ronald Coleman were among those who made a particular impact on me.

After my adventure in Czechoslovakia, I stayed with the Bertha Myers company, an amateur company, supported by the Inner London Education Authority, and played in the chorus of Euripides' *Alcestis* (crying throughout it – that's the effect great tragedy had on me until I learned to control my emotions!), in N.F. Simpson's surreal comedy, *A Resounding Tinkle*, and in *Oi!*, which we wrote ourselves – a play with music about the East End.

I did a succession of jobs – working at the Pru, at C & A for six months, where I modelled coats, as a receptionist and as a temp. I was encouraged by my drama teachers to go to drama school – other people from our group had gone on to RADA and other schools. I did a blitz on virtually every school before finally going to Webber Douglas. I was not the first East Ender to go there – Angela Lansbury was among a number of distinguished East End-born graduates of Webber Douglas. And I was far from being the first East Ender to go on the stage: the theatrical tradition is stronger there than anywhere in England, and its roots go back further.

Way back in the sixteenth century, the City of London forbade theatrical performances within its walls. They seemed to have thought of the theatre in the same way as they thought of other trades – the 'not

Street performers in Brick Lane.

in my back yard!' attitude that banished various obnoxious industries to the East End, and then exploited them. The theatre was no different: in 1576 a carpenter's son and actor, James Burbage, leased a patch of land off Shoreditch High Street, at the corner of Great Eastern Street and New Inn Yard, where Holywell Lane is now, and set up London's first permanent theatre – imaginatively calling it 'The Theatre'. It was soon followed by 'The Curtain' in Curtains Road, off Holywell Lane. Both were temporarily closed soon afterwards because of an outbreak of the plague, but when they reopened they were enormously popular – so much so that many clergymen preached against them, jealous of the audiences they attracted which contrasted with their own paltry congregations. Their appeal was more than just dramatic – this was a fringe area, noted for its many brothels and ale houses, and the theatres attracted boisterous crowds of drunks and tarts. Shakespeare arrived in London in about 1586 and probably worked with The Chamberlain's Men, a company of actors based at The Curtain, and while there wrote his first works, *Venus and Adonis* and *The Rape of Lucrece*. In 1598, The Theatre was dismantled and its wood was taken across the Thames and used to build the famous Globe Theatre on Bankside. The Curtain was disused by 1625 and burned down in the Great Fire of 1666.

That was only the beginning of East End theatre, and many more were built over the following years. Goodman's Fields Theatre in

Leman Street, Whitechapel, was converted from a shop in 1729. In 1733 it was moved to new premises in Ayliffe Street – it even had the same architect as Covent Garden. The famous actor David Garrick's debut was at Goodman's Fields, where he appeared as Richard III in 1741.

Alongside formal theatres, there were also a large number of gin palaces in East End that provided entertainment, but which were no better than brothels. Known as 'penny gaffs', they were gradually superseded by music halls such as the Royalty. Charrington, in his attempts to stamp out vice, tried to have many music halls closed – to the extent that the management of Lusby's in the Mile End Road (formerly the Eagle Tavern, and once the largest music hall in London) took action to prevent him distributing anti-vice tracts outside.

The Royalty Theatre, Wellclose Square, was opened in 1787 and burnt down in 1826. The Brunswick was built on the site in seven months – rather too hastily, as it turned out. During rehearsals three days after it was opened, on 28 February 1828, it collapsed, killing several actors, technicians, the proprietor and a passing team of horses! Wellclose Square's third theatre, Wilton's – named after its owner, a former Bath publican called John Wilton – was opened in 1859. Its foundation stone declared:

To Great Apollo, God of early morn. . .
We consecrate this shrine of gentle music.

The East End had long attracted theatre-goers from the West End, 'slumming it'. On Wilton's opening night, lines of cabs filled with West End toffs stretched back to St Paul's. They marvelled at the luxury of Wilton's – its vast 'Sunburner' chandelier had no fewer than 300 burners and 300 crystals. Great music hall entertainers of the calibre of George Leybourne appeared there: he earned the then staggering amount of £100 a night singing such songs as 'Champagne Charlie' – about a chap who drinks only champagne with friends *From Dukes and Lords, to cabmen down,* and *From Coffee and from Supper Rooms/ From Poplar to Pall Mall* – songs that emphasised the Cockney's disregard of any sort of class barrier.

Like other East End music halls, Wilton's developed a reputation for drunken and bawdy behaviour – prostitutes were said to lure sailors there, get them drunk and rob them; their victims were then dropped through a trapdoor, dragged down a passage and dumped in the neighbouring streets. Following a fire, it was closed in August 1880 – and, rather incongruously, became a Wesleyan mission, then in the 1950s a rag warehouse. In 1965 it was acquired by the Greater London Council and was used for various purposes, including the BBC's filming of *Bleak House* and as the setting for the video of Frankie Goes to Hollywood's song, *Relax*. An appeal launched by the London Music Hall Trust, with the support of such stars as Liza Minnelli, Lord Olivier and Roy Hudd, aims to restore Wilton's as part of a £10 million theme park, a national variety centre with London's oldest music hall at its heart.

Even music hall entertainers who didn't actually hail from the East End always regarded East End audiences as the most appreciative – and the most demanding: if an East Ender didn't think much of a per-

The East End theatre, yesterday and today.

QUEENS THEATRE
Poplar High Street
'Phone : EAST 3393

MONDAY TO FRIDAY
Continuous from 6.20
Two Full Performances

SATURDAY: 2 Distinct
Houses 6.15 and 8.20
BOOK YOUR SEATS

BOOKING OFFICE OPEN:
Mon. to Fri. 10.30 to 2 p.m.
Then at Stalls Pay Box
6.30 to 8.30
Saturday 10.30 to 8.0

★

PROGRAMME
2ᴰ

Week commencing
MONDAY : FEBRUARY 18th
1952

In accordance with the requirements of the L.C.C.:—
(1) The public may leave at the end of the performance or exhibition by all exit doors and such doors must at that time be open.
(2) All gangways, corridors, staircases and external passages intended for exit shall be kept entirely free from obstruction, whether permanent or temporary.
(3) Persons shall not be permitted to stand or sit in any of the other gangways. If standing intersecting the seating or to sit in any of the other gangways. If standing be permitted in the gangways at the sides and rear of the seating, it shall be limited to the numbers indicated in the notices exhibited in those positions
(4) The safety curtain must be lowered and raised in the presence of each audience.

In the interest of public health, Jeye's disinfectant is used in this theatre

PAVILION THEATRE

STRATFORD
EMPIRE

PROGRAMME

2ᴰ

formance, he wasn't shy about letting the artiste know! Songwriters went out of their way to come up with songs that appealed to Cockney sentiments. Harry Champion, whose food songs have already been mentioned, also sang 'Any Old Iron' and 'I'm 'Enery the Eighth I Am'; Albert Chevalier, whose most famous song was 'My Old Dutch', performed as a Cockney costermonger; Gus Elen's Cockney character performances included the song 'If it Wasn't for the 'ouses in Between', which contains the lines, *Wiv a ladder and some glasses/You could see to 'Ackney Marshes,/If it wasn't for the 'ouses in between*; Marie Lloyd, famous for her risqué act and such songs as 'The Old Cock Linnet', 'A Little of What you Fancy' and 'One of the Ruins that Cromwell Knocked About a Bit', lived for a time at 55 Graham Road, E8.

A number of music hall songs are specifically set in the East End, among them 'Burlington Bertie from Bow' by William Hargreaves. Dating from 1915, it was popularised by the male impersonator, Ella Shields:

I'm Burlington Bertie
I rise at ten thirty
And saunter along like a toff.
I walk down the Strand
With my gloves on my hand,
Then I walk down again with them off.
I'm all airs and graces, correct easy paces,
Without food so long I've forgot where my face is.
I'm Bert, Bert, I haven't a shirt,
But my people are well off you know!
Nearly everyone knows me from Smith to Lord Roseb'ry
I'm Burlington Bertie from Bow!

The song also contains the oddly prophetic lines:

I'm Bert, Bert and Royalty's hurt
When they ask me to dine, I say 'No!'
I've just had a banana with Lady Diana
I'm Burlington Bertie from Bow!

Then there is 'Two Lovely Black Eyes' by Charles Coborn:

Strolling so happy down Bethnal Green,
This gay youth you might have seen,
Tomkins and I with his girl between,
Oh what a surprise . . . !
I praised the Conservatives frank and free,
Tomkins got angry so speedily,
All in a moment he handed to me
   Two lovely black eyes.
   Two lovely black eyes!
   Oh what a surprise!
   Only for telling a man he was wrong,
   Two lovely black eyes.

Remembering the old songs at the Darby and Joan Club, Deancross Street.

The traditional 'knees-up' – I'm following in Mum's footsteps.

Then he goes on to argue the Liberal, Gladstone's cause, but unfortunately the man he discusses it with is a Tory, who also gives him 'two lovely black eyes'. Having learnt his lesson, like any sensible East Ender, he concludes it's best to 'leave it to others to fight it out'!

Even today, whenever East Enders get together round a piano, someone is sure to suggest singing some of these old favourites. I have sung some of them myself, and in one of my stage performances I sang music hall songs like 'The Boy I Love is Up in the Gallery' and 'Waiting at the Church'.

Among the many East End theatres that were but are no more – as a result of changing fashions, bombing or whatever – were the Temple of Harmony and the Pavilion, Whitechapel, which opened in 1856, became a Yiddish theatre, then operated as a cinema until 1934 and was demolished in 1956; the Standard, which presented Shakespeare and farces – sometimes on the same bill! – and Feinman's Yiddish People's Theatre, which opened in 1912 but closed soon afterwards.

The Three Cups in Bow Road, a lively music hall from 1855 to 1889, became a cinema in 1923; today there is a block of flats on the site.

As I mentioned earlier, I was often taken to variety shows at the Hackney Empire. My grandfather, Bill, seemed to know everyone in the East End, and when he took the family to the Hackney Empire, seemed only to nod to the commissionaire for us to be shown to the best seats or to a box. I'm happy to see that the Hackney Empire is back in business. Nowadays places like the Theatre Royal, Stratford East, built in 1884, and taken over in 1953 by Joan Littlewood's Theatre Workshop, stage a wide range of plays and such East End musicals as *Fings Ain't Wot They Used t'Be*.

Other active East End theatres included the Aldwych, Kingsland Road, and the Cambridge, Shoreditch (the Norfolk Village pub at 199 Shoreditch High Street was the bar of the theatre). The Half Moon Theatre (213 Mile End Road, E1) has spawned the Half Moon Young People's Theatre in Derbyshire Street. There is also the Curtain Theatre, (26 Commercial Street, E1).

I have already mentioned such well-known East End stars as Angela Lansbury and Jack Warner. The area has also produced such diverse talents as Terence Stamp, George Innes, Lee Montague, Georgia Brown, Kenny Lynch and Bernard Bresslaw.

Alfie Bass was born in Bethnal Green, Denis Norden in Hackney and Des O'Connor in Stepney. Bud Flanagan of Flanagan and Alan and other members of the Crazy Gang were born in Whitechapel. Like him, Tommy Trinder grew up in the music hall tradition, while Stanley Holloway, who was born in Manor Park, as a boy used to sing at the People's Palace and worked at Billingsgate. The story continues up to the present: David Essex, an East End docker's son, was discovered playing at The Eagle in Stratford.

As well as performers, the East End is noted for its playwrights such as Wolf Mankowitz, who was born in Bethnal Green and wrote such East End Jewish plays as *The Bespoke Overcoat*, musicals such as *Make Me an Offer* and numerous screenplays. Arnold Wesker, who was born in Stepney, wrote *Chicken Soup and Barley*, which is set in Stepney Green at the time of the Fascist marches. Actor/playwright Harold Pinter was born in the East End and went to the same school in Hackney as another of my favourite writers, Steven Berkoff, the author of *East*, *Decadence* and other hard-hitting plays. East Ender Johnny Speight created the character of Alf Garnett in *Till Death Us Do Part*, and plays like Jack Rosenthal's *The Evacuees* have looked to the East End for their inspiration.

Impresarios including Lord Delfont and Lew and Leslie Grade were born in the East End. Lew's nephew Michael Grade was Head of Light Entertainment at the BBC when *EastEnders* was launched.

Ever since the 1919 film, *A Murder in Limehouse*, the East End has served as an evocative film location, its dockland warehouses featuring in such films as *The Long Good Friday*. The film, *To Sir, With Love*, was set in the East End. It has always been a source for actors – scouts even came to my school once looking for suitable East End urchins to appear in the film production of *Oliver!*

An East End street party for the Coronation. Even the children wore red, white and blue dresses!

144

Alongside the performing arts, the activity that has long excited East Enders is boxing. At the famous Repton Boys Club, and in places like it scattered throughout the East End, boys have learned to box partly for recreation, partly in order to be able to defend themselves should the occasion arise. Many Jewish boys took up boxing in the 1930s to defend themselves against the blackshirts, some of them going on to become famous professional fighters. Before the pop music scene, boxing was one of the few acceptable ways in which a young East Ender could achieve wealth and status. Jack Solomons, a Hackney fishmonger, promoted boxing at the Devonshire Sporting Club, becoming the leading boxing promoter in Britain. The list of his proteges and other notable East End boxers is endless: Jack 'Kid' Berg, Harry Mizler, Ted 'Kid' Lewis, Daniel Mendoza, Dave Finn, the Corbett and Danahar brothers from Bethnal Green, Billy Walker from West Ham, and Charlie Magri.

East End boxing matches are enjoyed as much for their audiences as for the sport: they are noted for shouting such humorous comments as 'Stop it ref, they're killing each other!' – before a single punch has been landed!

Wrestling is also popular among East Enders, as are all traditional working-class sporting pursuits – football, darts, snooker and billiards, horse and dog racing. Less well known is how much American basketball owes to an East Ender! Abe Sapperstein, founder of the Harlem Globetrotters, the black American basketball team, was born in Spitalfields in 1908, later emigrating to the USA.

The East End has also been the venue for many productions of a more cultural nature: it has been the source of inspiration for many artists – Turner often painted Thames scenes here, as did James Whistler, whose pictures of Wapping, painted in 1860-4, are among his best. David Bomberg's *Mud Baths* represents the old Turkish Baths in Brick Lane; Mark Gertler, who lived at 32 Elder Street in Spitalfields, was so poor that his first pictures were done on the paving stones of Whitechapel; book illustrators including Phil May, Thomas Heath Robinson and Pearl Binder produced many evocative drawings of East End scenes. Even the Blitz inspired artists: Graham Sutherland's wonderful 1941 painting, *Devastation: an East End Street*, can be seen in the Tate Gallery, and Henry Moore drew amazing pictures of people sheltering. Hugh Easton's stained glass at St Dunstan's of the blitzed Stepney rising from the ashes is particularly beautiful. Many photographers have found richness in the East End: policeman turned photographer John Topham produced a marvellous record of East End life in the 'thirties, Boris Bennett of Whitechapel was one of the best portrait photographers of his day, and Lord Snowdon's pictures of down-and-outs were among the most memorable images of more recent times.

The list of books about the East End is enormous. Needless to say, both in true and fictitious accounts, many of them have focussed on the poverty and deprivation of the area, and have depressing titles like *In Darkest London*, *This Gutter Life* or *The Bitter Cry of Outcast London*. Henry Mayhew wrote a series of articles for the *Morning*

Chronicle which were later published as a book, *London Labour and the London Poor* (1851), revealing many of the problems of the poor of the East End. Jack London, American author of *The People of the Abyss* (1903), actually disguised himself as a down-and-out in order to infiltrate East End slums to research and write his revealing documentary account of East End low life, producing statistics that showed that 55 per cent of children in East End died before the age of five, compared with 18 per cent in the West End.

Some of these books were actually quite influential: Arthur Morrison, who was born in Poplar in 1863, published two East End novels, *Tales of Mean Streets* in 1894 and *A Child of the Jago* in 1896. He stayed with the vicar of Holy Trinity Shoreditch, Arthur Osborne Jay, and was introduced by him to Old Nichol Street, the area with the highest incidence of crime and infant mortality in London. Calling it the 'Jago', Morrison used it as the setting for his 'story of a boy who, but for his environment, would have been a good citizen'. Jay had been battling for slum clearance for years, but it was due to the popularity and impact of *A Child of the Jago* that the work was finally done and in 1900 a new housing estate was opened by the Prince of Wales.

There are, finally, many poems about the East End, but few as poignant as *In Limehouse*. It comes as something of a surprise to discover that it was written by Clement Atlee, the first Labour mayor of Stepney and the first Labour Prime Minister:

In Limehouse, in Limehouse, before the break of day,
I hear the feet of many men who go upon their way,
Who wander through the City,
The grey and cruel City,
Through streets that have no pity,
The streets where men decay.

In Limehouse, in Limehouse, by night as well as day,
I hear the feet of children who go to work or play,
Of children born to sorrow,
The workers of tomorrow
How shall they work tomorrow
Who get no bread today?

In Limehouse, in Limehouse, today and every day
I see the weary mothers who sweat their souls away:
Poor, tired mothers, trying
To hush the feeble crying
Of little babies dying
For want of bread today.

In Limehouse, in Limehouse, I'm dreaming of the day
When evil time shall perish and be driven clean away,
When father, child and mother
Shall live and love each other,
And brother help his brother
In happy work and play.

EastEnders
And The Changing
East End

E VER since *EastEnders* started, people have been asking where it is
filmed and if it is an accurate portrayal of life in the 'real East
End'. The answer to the first question is that Albert Square does
not exist. Neither does the 'London Borough of Walford' in which
it is supposed to be situated, nor even its postcode, 'E20'. There is an
Albert Square in Stratford, on the fringe of the East End, and there is an
Albert Gardens, a pretty street of recently renovated houses off the
Commercial Road in Stepney. Albert Square in *EastEnders* is a
specially-built set at the Elstree Studios. When the set – which is a
permanent construction and one of the largest ever built for a British
television production – was being designed, researchers and photographers visited some of the Victorian squares in the East End, particularly in Hackney and Bethnal Green, and scrupulously copied
architectural details. The result is a composite of East End buildings,
the sort of mixture you might find anywhere in the East End – a corner
shop, a pub, an off-licence, a launderette, Victorian houses and tower
blocks. When the series started, researchers even went to the trouble
of visiting East End markets and shops to ensure that the actors were
wearing the right clothes.

The casting is every bit as meticulous: many of the actors are, like
me, East Enders: Anna Wing, who plays Lou Beale, is from Hackney;
Ethel Skinner (Gretchen Franklin) is an East Ender, and those who are
not tend to come from other parts of London and are familiar with East
End life and the Cockney accent. I joined the cast just as the filming
started, with a three month contract and an option for a further year.

Living in the East End, I know people like the characters in *East-
Enders.* There is an authenticity about the way in which the programme reflects contemporary developments: the casting of Colin, the

gay 'Yuppie' designer, better off than most, who lives in a high-tech flat and can afford to employ a cleaner, is very true to life, as all over the East End there are such people moving into traditional communities. The ethnic mix is also accurately represented: just as in the 'real' East End, we have not only the long-established families such as the Beales and the Fowlers but also the West Indian Carpenters, Ali the Turkish Cypriot, the Jewish doctor Harold Legg and the Indian Naima.

Because our lives are crammed into two half-hour programmes a week, there is more drama and incident than there might be in your average East End street, but the problems they depict are those of working-class communities everywhere – family problems, financial difficulties, crime. This brings out into an open forum for discussion questions on otherwise taboo subjects, such as divorce, suicide and mental illness. It makes people think and talk – many children write to me, and some English teachers have used *EastEnders* as a means of firing their classes with enthusiasm to discuss or write about all manner of important themes.

Compared with other long-running TV or radio series, *EastEnders* is relatively young. As yet we have not faced some of the problems that shows such as *Coronation Street* and *The Archers* have found in achieving continuity: for example, if someone appears in one episode driving a car and then in a later episode mentions that they can't drive, droves of faithful followers of the programme would be puzzled and many of them would write in to point out the inconsistency. Someone evidently did this so often with *Coronation Street* that he was eventually offered the job of 'historian' of the series, and *The Archers* has always kept a detailed card index itemising every little aspect of each character's personality, his likes and dislikes, whether or not he wears glasses, and so on.

Some people may dismiss the programme as portraying an East End that is nothing like the East End they knew. Others have leapt to its defence, though, reminding us that *EastEnders* is not an historical series. It doesn't attempt to show what the East End was like a generation or more ago, but what it is like today, and, for better or for worse, the East End has changed.

Whenever I hear anyone talking about the East End I feel a tingle down my spine, and I think to myself, 'That's my home!' However, though I strongly believe that a consciousness of one's roots is vital, it is equally important to accept that change is inevitable. I loved my childhood, and I revel in my memories of it – but I don't want to remain a child. Then was then and now is now, and though I loved the East End as it was, I also love the East End as it is, and I am sure I always will.

Index

Acknowledgements

The publishers wish to thank Chris Steele-Perkins, Magnum Photos Limited, for taking the majority of the specially commissioned photographs. Thanks go also to the following copyright holders for their permission to reproduce the illustrations listed below:

BBC Hulton Picture Library pp. 34/5, 48, 51, 58 (bottom), 59, 66, 90, 91 (bottom), 144; Mike Busselle (frontispiece), pp. 9, 86; Camera Press Limited p. 54; Anita Dobson pp. 10, 12, 13, 14, 15, 16, 17, 19, 20, 21, 22, 23, 25, 142; David Drummond pp. 138/9; Mary Evans Picture Library p. 29; Eugene Fleury p. 26; Hackney Archives pp. 62/3; London Transport Museum pp. 42, 43, 60; Brian and Sally Shuel pp. 96, 97; Edwin Smith p. 116; Topham Picture Library pp. 38 (top), 47 (top), 60, 64, 65, 73, 84, 85, 114/115, 123; Tower Hamlets Local History Library pp. 30, 31, 45, 50 (top), 58 (top), 78/9, 82 (bottom), 106, 138/9; Joe Wright pp. 126, 127, 129, 130, 131, 133. Aerial photography preceding title-page supplied by Aerofilms Limited, Gate Studios, Station Road, Boreham Wood, Herts.